FAITH IT
Till You Make It

FAITH IT
Till You Make It

How to Build Your Faith One Doubt at a Time

Reverend Bernardo Monserrat

Health Communications, Inc.
Deerfield Beach, Florida

www.hci-online.com

Library of Congress Cataloging-in-Publication Data

Monserrat, Bernardo
Faith it till you make it : how to build your faith one doubt at a time / Bernardo Monserrat.
p. cm.
ISBN 0-7573-0003-0 (tp)
1. United Church of Religious Science–Doctrines. I. Title.

BP605.U53 M66 2002
299'.93–dc21 2002068471

ISBN 0-7573-0003-0

Publisher: Health Communications, Inc.
3201 S.W. 15th Street
Deerfield Beach, FL 33442-8190

Cover and inside book design by Lawna Patterson Oldfield
Cover photo ©Comstock Images

To Catherine,
whose faith in me
is the light that guides my way.

CONTENTS

ACKNOWLEDGMENTS

In deep gratitude to Gary Seidler whose faith in me manifested in his heartfelt emotional and financial support. Thanks to Dr. Marcia Sutton and Reverend Eric Strom whose creativity stimulated my own. Their ministry, Sacred Days (*www.SacredDays.org*), is an inspiration. Thanks to Reverend Mary Murray Shelton, Reverend Donald Victor Morgan, Dr. Herbert E. Beatty, Dr. Catherine Monserrat, Mary Jackson, Barbara Sandoval and Mary Beth Bigger, who reviewed the manuscript and gave loving feedback; to Reverend Petra Weldes, Dr. Dan Montgomery and Maeileen Tuffi for their mentoring; and to Barbara Doern Drew who edited the manuscript. Finally, to all of my students who inspired me to write it.

INTRODUCTION

The faith that stands on authority is not faith.
The reliance on authority measures
the withdrawal of the soul.

—Ralph Waldo Emerson

What would life be like if we confronted each fork in the road with the certainty that either path we chose would be magnificent? What level of happiness could we attain by relaxing into the moment? What would it be like not to have to plan our future or review our past? How would it feel to realize success in all our endeavors? Are you intrigued by these possibilities? Well, you can *faith it until you make it.* That's right. There is a way to believe—to have *faith*—and to live that can help you turn these possibilities into realities. There is no magical process involved here, however. Achieving this kind of faith requires vision, work and perseverance.

Through personal experiences, I have observed many people who developed such a faith and who accomplished many of their dreams. In fact, it is possible to live in such a faith-filled mental state that we can be assured of positive outcomes throughout our lives. Most importantly, when we achieve this state of being, we can make a powerful difference in both our lives and the lives of those around us. Since beginning my study of metaphysical religions and philosophies, I have often come across the refrain, "Fake it until you make it." This gross misinterpretation of a positive outlook on life has left me wondering how to best teach students the elusive concept of faith. To believe that our lives will turn out for the good requires more than mere "faking" or pretending. We may pretend for a lifetime and yet never "make it." A positive outlook on life must be grounded in philosophy, a useful psychology and a practical spirituality. Anything less than that is just "faking it."

For over ten years I have attempted to teach my students about the nature of God, faith and the divine creative process. Every time I start a class, I acknowledge the frustration that we will face. We bring different belief systems—even different words—to the discussion. Most frustrating is the fact that we attempt to define "something" that has no definition. I tell my students that embarking on such a paradoxical journey requires faith.

As a minister, I am expected to give information that instills faith in others. It is not an easy task. Many students come to me with their faith in tatters—they feel hopeless and see nothing but a bleak future before them. I often wish I had a magic potion that would restore such people's faith—but I don't.

It has been my personal and professional experience, however, that when faith is "practiced" it builds in strength. Moreover, when faith is strong, it isn't "lost" as often. My belief in the reality of faith building led me to write this book, which is a road map for the practice and development of faith.

Faith, like God, is ultimately indefinable, but I use many near-definitions and metaphors throughout this text that may be helpful to you. I am comfortable in saying that for me, *Faith is a mental attitude that encourages us to overcome seeming obstacles and disillusionments.* Faith is the mental "substance" that drives us beyond our comfort levels and places us in new creative ventures; and it is the emotional "potion" that soothes and heals our wounded hearts.

When my wife, Catherine, and I completed our studies in Seattle, Washington, we began an inner search for where we wished to practice our careers. We prayed, allowed the vision to emerge, made lists of our preferences, made more lists of possibilities, visited options and discussed probabilities. The result of that arduous effort was choosing to build a life in Santa Fe, New Mexico. There was a slight problem, however: There were three ministers already covering that particular pulpit.

When faith is high, it is easy to neglect details, so we disregarded the pulpit's occupancy rate and, like gold rushers heading for pay dirt, decided to go anyway. We quit our jobs, sold our beautiful townhouse that overlooked the beach in West Seattle, packed a moving van and headed for the southernmost corner of the Rocky Mountains. Many say that Santa Fe, the "City Different," is not a destination but a process. How right they are.

Without a job to do, it did not take me long to get depressed. I felt confused, betrayed and angry. My faith quickly sank in a morass of idleness. Unemployment did not suit me—I had always done better with a paycheck and a title. I had been well trained to "do," but not to "be." In fact, as far as I knew, to "be" was simply "*not* to be." Being stripped of my old ways of thinking, however, was exactly what the "doctor" ordered.

As my faith began to vanish, I hit a spiritual bottom and reached out for help. I started getting assistance from family, friends and teachers. My previous training and discipline in spiritual practices helped bolster my weakened spiritual resources. Most important, I became open to and accepted guidance. I learned a lesson in humility, and then I implemented a plan of action. Slowly, I regained my faith.

I appeared at the church one morning to volunteer my services. I was assigned the receptionist's duties. Although it was not what I initially had in mind, it was clearly what Providence had in mind. In retrospect, I have come to understand that humility is an essential component of a healthy ministry. I am sure I could not have learned the lessons I did in any other way. That same week, I was also hired as the youth minister. Within a span of four months, all of the ministers resigned. I was then asked to be the interim minister while the congregation sought a permanent replacement. At the end of that process, I was offered the position of senior minister, and I humbly accepted. My faith had won out, but there were some precious lessons along the way.

This book starts from the premise that faith is a natural state. It is our divine inheritance, if you will—our original blessing. Though it can be lost, it can also be regained. It evolves and grows through education and practice, and an educated faith can sustain us through many challenging situations. If we persist in practicing our faith and educating ourselves, faith may also become enlightened. This type of faith, though rare, is available to us all, even if for the briefest of moments. Once we have experienced enlightened faith, we will remain on our spiritual path, seeking a repeat experience. I will often talk about spiritual practices. These are mental and physical exercises designed to bolster our faith. These include prayer, meditation, contemplation, walks in nature, inspirational readings, rituals, religious education, prayer groups, journaling, creative arts, Twelve-Step groups, conversations with God (silent or aloud), chanting, yoga and any other activity that leads to communion with that which is larger than we are.

I will tell you stories from my life, as well as from the lives of my family, friends and students, and share with you the lessons we all learned along the way. It was through the observation of such real-life faith experiences that I came to formulate the "Evolution of Faith" matrix (see chapter 1) and its four stages, which form the foundation of this book.

The stories in this book are personal. They are factual and fractal. They exist in my memory and in my soul. They have one theme and a thousand pieces. In coming together, they are a blend of truth and legend. I tell them as I best remember them, but I see them through the gyroscope of the heart. These are the stories that have shaped my life. We are all composites of fact and fiction, history and myth. When you read them, feel what resonates true for you. It is at that point that these stories will touch your soul and fire your faith.

The quote by Ralph Waldo Emerson is from a book called *The Gospel of Emerson.* Emerson has been an important teacher in my life, and his words remain one of the main sources of my personal philosophy. *The Gospel* is a compilation of quotes from Emerson's major works, distilled into several main themes. The book was composed by Newton Dillaway and is published by Unity Books, Unity Village, Missouri 64065.

In Spanish there is a saying for when things start to unravel: *Ay, Dios mio!* This is the best prayer I know. *Ay* ("ouch!") lets out the pain. *Dios* ("God") summons the boss. *Mio* ("mine") defines my role. I am indeed the one who must do the work. Enlightened faith doesn't just "happen." It requires discipline and commitment. You need the right tools and experienced help to guide you along the way. May this book serve you well, and may it be as much fun for you to read as it was for me to write. *Que Dios te bendiga.* ("May God bless you.")

CHAPTER ONE

What Is Faith?

We do not guess today the mood, the pleasure, the power of tomorrow when we are building up our being. Of lower states, of acts of routine and sense, we can tell somewhat; but the masterpieces of God, the total growths and universal movements of the soul, he hideth; they are incalculable.

—*Ralph Waldo Emerson*

Would you like enough faith to move mountains or part the seas? What about enough faith to get you through a serious illness or the loss of a loved one? Could you use more faith when you contemplate a job change or wrestle with a bout of depression? We all would like an extra dose of this elusive elixir that seems to hide when we need it most. Yet, if we are to find faith, we must first know what it is.

There is no *one* way to describe faith. Actually, faith cannot be defined. Only approximations can be made. These approximations are personal and subjective, but very real. Every one of us knows when we are feeling hopeless and pessimistic about the outcome of our lives. We all know what discouragement feels like. Most important, we can observe the behaviors that are the result of such feelings. These behaviors can be tracked and labeled. By tracking our feelings and behaviors and giving them names, we can readily see that faith is not an "either/or" proposition but rather a continuum. In other words, we can be more or less hopeful at a particular time in our lives. Our optimism may be higher on one day than it is on another. Paradoxically, our faith can be strong in one specific area of our lives, but weak in another. All of this points to the phenomenon that faith can be affected—increased or decreased—according to a variety of factors.

We will study that phenomenon throughout this book. We will learn what faith is, and how it can be affected and influenced by our intellect and our emotions. We will learn that faith is an innate gift that can evolve through education, practice and commitment. And we will come to know that hope and optimism are not dependent on external circumstances. We are not victims. We are not at the mercy of the life that surrounds us.

The Evolution of Faith Matrix

Our primary learning tool will be the "Evolution of Faith" matrix (see page 4). I developed the matrix and its four stages after being inspired by the groundbreaking work of Marsha Sutton and Eric Stom. The top of the matrix shows the four different stages of faith: natural, lost, educated and enlightened. There is a chapter dedicated to each stage. The columns of the matrix describe the behavioral, mental and emotional components of each faith stage for ten categories of spiritual growth: deity identity, emotional response, intellectual activity, mental participation, innate reaction, probability factor, religious tools, causality, divine involvement and reactive pattern. In this chapter, I explain why these categories are important for the student who is interested in personal and spiritual growth.

What I have tried to show with the matrix is that faith does not have an "on/off" switch—though it may sometimes feel that way. Faith actually falls along a continuum. It can be built over time and with practice. The matrix can be used in two ways: to identify spiritual progress and to guide you along the steps to spiritual growth. Let's take a moment to review the categories.

EVOLUTION OF FAITH MATRIX

Categories	Natural	Lost	Educated	Enlightened
Deity Identity	God as Person	God Is Absent	God as Partner	God as Presence
Emotional Response	Hope	Fear	Trust	Surrender
Intellectual Activity	Pleading	Blaming	Affirming	Awareness/ Mindfulness
Mental Participation	Vision	Ignorance	Realization	Revelation
Innate Reaction	Instinctual	Desperate	Intellectual	Intuitive
Probability Factor	Chance	Doubt	Cause and Effect	Connectivity/ Synchronicity
Religious Tools	Request/ Prayer	Cursing	Treatment or Scientific Prayer	Contemplation
Causality	Expectations	Worry	Expectancy	Knowing
Divine Involvement	Probable	Darkness	Law	Grace
Reactive Pattern	Resignation	Feeling Victimized	Responsibility	Blissful

- **Deity identity** is our concept of God. Often this is unconscious and may vary from time to time depending on our life situation.
- **Emotional response** is our internal feeling or reaction to a particular faith stage.
- **Intellectual activity** is how we think during different faith stages.
- **Mental participation** is our mind's reaction to a faith stage. (Please note that I am making a distinction between *thinking* and *mind*. Mind encompasses thinking, but is much more. For instance, *ignorance* is not a thought, but a state of mind from which we think.)
- **Innate reactions** are psycho-spiritual responses to our situations. They are mindful responses of the intellect and heart. Some would say that innate reactions are the pulsations of the soul, or that psychic endeavor that connects us to something larger than ourselves.
- **Probability factor** is the manner in which our mind connects our mental states and is manifested in our life.
- **Religious tools** are the different activities or behaviors that connect our *intellectual activity* with our *Deity identity*.

- **Causality** is the manner in which our *mental states* connect with our level of faith. For instance, if I am applying for a job and my faith is low, I may be less than confident about getting the job. If my faith is high, however, I will have inspired expectations about being hired.
- **Divine involvement** is how the *Deity identity* moves in our lives according to our level of faith.
- **Reactive pattern** is our general demeanor, both mental and emotional, during a particular stage of faith.

These terms will become clearer as we use them through examples and stories.

Our Natural Faith

Each of us comes into this life with God's imprint. Call it our soul. This soul can be expressed through the way we live. We make the choice whether to allow its expression or not. Faith is the soul's desire to have us fully express who and what we are intended to be. Once the soul's desire is obtained, bliss is the payoff. I believe that faith is a gift we receive at our conception. We are born with it, and we can tap into it at any time.

Nothing and no one can take away our natural faith but ourselves. Unfortunately, we often give it away. We give it to our parents soon after our birth. We are completely dependent on them for our welfare, and we redefine our faith based on this childhood dependency. Our early impressions and beliefs continue to influence our everyday perceptions and decisions later in life.

Our natural faith is childlike. It defines God as a person. We attribute magic and overwhelming power to this figure. We also give God a personality not unlike that of our parents. Our natural faith usually has us feeling optimistic and hopeful. We have positive visions of our future, and we often interact with our person-God through prayers that are really requests, hoping to catch God in a benevolent mood!

At this stage of natural faith, we often plead with, (request) our God for improved conditions. That is our intellectual activity. Based on that intellectual activity —pleading—what we believe will be the outcome of our request is based on "chance." Consequently, our lives are motivated by one expectation after another, and disappointment often becomes part of the "way life is." We tend to place our faith in upcoming events. We pray these will enhance our well-being, and we have a great deal of hope and optimism around a specific result. At this level of faith, we believe that God's involvement in our lives is probable. We are not certain, but we figure that there is a good chance God is "around." We lose nothing by praying. We say, "If all else fails, try prayer." Our typical reaction is one of resignation. We come to accept our lot in life, but not without complaints.

For several years I worked with a client who initially could only complain about his life. He had been raised in a religion that personified God, a restrictive religion that provided few choices for his life. His entire family was involved in it, and if he wanted to be a part of that family, he did not have much spiritual choice. He had to abide by his religion's tenets. When he came to see me, he was recently divorced, suicidal and in a serious midlife crisis. When I first started working with him, I assumed that the healing would evolve easily. I would encourage him to grieve the loss of his marriage, and he would then be on his way. However, when I took his history, I learned that his mother had died when he was a young boy. This happened although his religion had assured him that if he prayed the right way and diligently enough, his mother would be spared from her illness. His feelings of betrayal went unheeded, and his faith never developed.

He had struggled through adulthood with a great deal

of support from his wife and family. Never having developed self-autonomy, he grappled with decisions by not making them. He mainly depended on others to set the course of his life, and if things didn't work out, he complained. He moved from "job to job and town to town," until his midlife crisis and subsequent divorce.

During our sessions, I created a safe environment where he could complain to his heart's content. While his depression lasted, I simply listened to his life of woes. He was miserable, neither happy in his sinful affair, nor able to return to his family and religion. About a year into our work together, and with much encouragement on my part, he began to see that the helplessness he felt was due to his immature faith. He had not dared to question the faith that his religion had taught him. That, plus the trauma of his mother's death, had him stuck in a childish relationship with God. All he had been able to do was plead to an undependable God, and then complain when things did not go his way. In time, his natural faith was slowly restored and he immediately gained confidence in himself. He began to confront difficult situations, and he learned to express his desires with an eye for compromise. His ability to negotiate increased, and he ultimately made some decisions that improved his well-being as well as the lives of those around him.

When our natural faith is gone, we must question what has taken its place. We must place as much faith in our inner strength and capabilities as we do in the outer, infinite possibility for good. We must never cease searching for our faith. It is our most precious gift, and we should never surrender it to anyone or anything.

FAITH ENHANCER

Set aside some time to consider the following questions about your faith. You may want to write down your answers: Who first taught you about faith? Whom did you trust? When and how did you transfer your natural faith to God?

When Faith Is Lost

Our natural faith is often eroded or lost when stressful circumstances overwhelm us. It is important to remember, however, that although we may feel our faith has lessened or is even lost, it is still there and it is still faith. Something in us always wants to believe!

Natural faith doesn't leave us; it simply recedes for a while. When our faith is lost, we tend to deny God—although we may not say this aloud to others, or even to ourselves. Now our emotional response is fear and despair. We see ourselves as victims and blame others for our predicaments. Our religious tool (if you can call it that) may be a loud curse. Nevertheless, even a heartfelt "goddamn" still has the makings of a prayer!

When faith is lost, the probability factor or outcome of our praying is, at best, doubtful. We seem caught in a trap of not knowing what has caused our problems, and this ignorance further dissolves our relationship with God. There is darkness surrounding our connection with the divine.

When I was nineteen years old, I decided to leave my childhood religion. My departure was due partly to my rebellious period, but I was also seeking answers that the church officials could not supply. The straw that finally broke my religious back was a particular dogmatic decision that condemned to hell a close friend who had recently committed suicide.

Unfortunately, along with abandoning my religion, I decided to get rid of God. I had never made a distinction between religion and spirituality. An immense sense of freedom followed my decision, but it was also accompanied by a deep depression. Concurrently, I severed a long-standing relationship and decided to move away from my family. With all my props removed, I had no one but myself to lean on. My reliance on any higher power was gone. Soon I found drugs and alcohol to ease the pain. These provided short-term relief, but my depression grew. I became self-destructive and suicidal, and my friends began to worry about me. It became a challenge to make it to work with my hangovers. This ordeal lasted three years.

By "chance," a new neighbor moved next door. He was my age and already had a wife and children. Despite his responsibilities, this young man seemed at peace. He was self-confident and deliberate, and his life was manageable. I was immediately drawn to him, since he displayed the behavior and emotions that I was only able to experience when high or drunk. He began to educate me. He taught me some simple spiritual practices—deep breathing, yoga postures, gentle walks and meditation. He allowed me to go at my own pace and never pushed himself into my journey. I began to feel better and my drug and alcohol consumption started to decline. He said that, "Once you have planted the seed, all you have to do is watch it grow." And grow it did.

That was the first time I lost my faith and had to regain it on my own. In retrospect, I can see how my childhood faith was not supporting my spiritual development. Yet, the rediscovery of faith did not demand that I return to my childhood religion. My experience at nineteen taught me that religion and spirituality are not the same. I could have a strong and mature faith, but not belong to any particular religion. My newfound spiritual maturity also taught me that my life would be a journey, one of self-discovery and increased awareness of others. My education had just begun.

FAITH ENHANCER

Write in your journal about the first time that you had a serious loss of faith. Make your description as detailed as possible. Hopefully, this will bring completion to the experience and encourage the rebirth of a new opportunity for spirituality.

An Educated Faith

What I learned during that early period in my life was that our faith in God can be regained through support and education. We can learn about who and what God is, and how we can relate to God.

Whether we are aware of it or not, our faith matures as we learn to clearly perceive our outer circumstances and our inner capabilities—that is, the way we see the world and our ability to respond confidently to it. These perceptions are expressions of God, and they contribute to the belief systems that support our faith. Once we become "stuck" at a particular faith level, however, it is not easy to change these perceptions—even when we need to. Our perceptions, self-confidence and belief systems all work well until a particular event hits us over the head and sends us reeling for help.

Yet, it is not necessary to wait for an encounter with the proverbial two-by-four in order for our faith level to get a boost. With intention and discipline we can educate our faith. This education will be grounded in an intellectual study of God and the spiritual practices necessary to make us accessible to God. Let us turn to the Evolution of Faith matrix and see what an educated faith looks like.

With an educated faith, our perception of God has matured. *God is now a partner, someone or something that participates in our lives.* We come to understand that we have a cocreative relationship with God: God uses us as much as we use God. Our emotional response to this relationship is one of trust. We now rely on God, and we come to know how the divine works in our lives. This is what "law" means under divine involvement in the matrix. Our mental participation at this faith level involves the realization of, and insights into, this unique partnership. Our lives are no longer ruled by chance—they are the results of our own attitude, thoughts and actions. Prayer stops being a plea bargain and becomes an affirmation. We stop having specific wants and instead simply expect good. The challenge of this mature level of faith is that we must be willing to take responsibility for all aspects of our lives—not just the ones we like, but *all* the results that our thinking produces. This does not mean that we take blame or feel guilty. It means that we become "response-able."

Several years ago, my sister was diagnosed with a rare blood disease. It came as a shock, since she had always been healthy. The doctor told her that not much was known about it. In some individuals it developed into cancer, while in others it remained dormant. Although she could be asymptomatic, the disease could not be cured nor would it go away.

My sister had been a student of spirituality for many years and had redefined her childhood relationship to God. When the doctor recommended that they do chemotherapy, she opted against it. She told him that she wanted to try some things on her own. She decided to increase her spiritual practices by waking each morning before sunup and doing an hour of yoga. This was followed by time in meditation and spiritual readings. She lightened her workload and reduced stress levels. She made a commitment to follow her intuition and dedicate herself to a spiritual lifestyle. She attended our Sunday services regularly and participated in classes and retreats. She submerged herself in the education of her faith.

Over time, she returned to her doctor for biannual blood tests that showed some improvement but remained in the danger zone. The doctor would typically recommend chemotherapy, and she would habitually turn it down. This routine continued for a couple of years, with the blood tests being done less frequently. Then, at one of her yearly checkups, the blood tests were completely negative. The doctor silently stared at her results for a long time, then he looked her in the eyes and asked, "What is it that you have been doing all these years?" My sister had entered full recovery.

As an aside, I would like to emphasize that I tell the above story not to recommend faith-healing strategies in lieu of traditional medical interventions. I have helped many members of my congregation with their faith while they received medical treatment at the same time. To use one does not imply that you must abandon the other.

FAITH ENHANCER

Consider the following statements, and write down your reactions to them in your journal: When we practice an educated faith, we come to expect miracles. In fact, we come to believe that if miracles are not *happening, something is wrong.*

Enlightened Faith

I had a teacher in ministerial school who said, "When we get our relationships, finances and health in order, *that's* when the real work begins!" Though it may be difficult to imagine a time when these three major areas of our lives are in order, that is indeed the time when our spiritual work truly begins.

Enlightened faith is a mental and emotional state that defies definition. *It is perhaps a true state of divinity where there is no sense of separation from others or our environment. It is the feeling that all of our life has purpose.* Some mystics are able to describe this transcendental experience. Enlightened saints from both the East and the

West have pointed the way to this level of faith, and we have much to learn from studying their spiritual paths. When our faith is enlightened, we experience God as a presence, a constant that permeates all that we are and all that is. Our faith changes from a "faith in God" to a "faith of God," from believing in God to being of God. We see all of life as interconnected and having purpose—there are no accidents. Our awareness of this "synchronicity"—or divine order—rules our perceptions. At this faith level, our prayers are a continuous contemplation of what *is*. All that we do becomes a prayer. The awareness of God and goodness is constantly with us. *We suddenly "know" the rightness of everything in life, particularly* in our lives. We accept our time and place, and we surrender to every circumstance. God's involvement in our lives is pure grace, and we view life with awe.

I do not know many individuals who live an enlightened faith, at least not all of the time. I do have a few friends who are quite mystical, and they report experiencing moments of enlightenment. These are not "special" people, but they conduct themselves in a way that uplifts and enlarges those around them. They are ordinary folks conducting their lives with disciplined spirituality. They need less attention. Their personalities are uniform, as if all the rough edges had been scrubbed smooth. Little seems to rattle them, and they wear a half smile that invites the world to come in.

I make a habit of retreating into silence and isolation for a couple of weeks every year. During this period, I spend much time in meditation and contemplation. I make simple meals, spend time in nature, make my own music, write, play with my dog and pray. This annual retreat is essential to my lifestyle. On several occasions during these retreats, I have experienced moments of expanded consciousness. It is as though a switch is turned on, and I perceive my surroundings and my inner thoughts in a completely different manner.

The duration of these moments differs. Some last a few minutes, others a few hours. My hunch is that we all experience such states, if only for a few seconds. I am convinced that these moments of "enlightened faith" are what feed our souls and keep us alive.

FAITH ENHANCER

Endeavor to spend time every day in silent contemplation. Suspend mental activity and simply be with the moment. Refrain from judgments and simply witness what is so.

CHAPTER TWO

Our Natural Faith

> Of the perception now fast becoming a conscious fact, that there is One Mind, and that all the powers and privileges which lie in any, lie in all; that I, as a man, may claim and appropriate whatever of true or fair or good or strong has anywhere been exhibited; that Moses and Confucius, Montaigne and Leibnitz, are not so much individuals as they are parts of man and parts of me. . . .
>
> —*Ralph Waldo Emerson*

In chapter 1, we learned about the nature of faith and that ultimately, faith cannot be defined. Faith is a "state of mind" that waxes and wanes along a continuum. Faith can be lost and regained, and it can be educated and developed into an enlightened state. It is natural to want to gain mastery over our faith, to have a deep connection with it and be at its blessing, rather than its mercy. But we can't manipulate our faith. On the contrary, faith grows when we surrender.

Our Desire for the Next Breath

A few years ago, my wife and I were visiting Costa Rica. This Central American country, with its abundant flora and fauna, is dotted with deserted beaches. Being a bodysurfing enthusiast, I ached for a few good waves. At the sight of a spectacular sandy stretch, I rushed into the water without paying much attention to the surf. Suddenly I was surprised by a sizable wave that was crashing down on me at an unprecedented speed. With no time to jump out of its way, I dove under the wave to find protection. To my shock, the full force of its crest crashed onto my back. It pounded me into the sandy bottom, knocking the wind out of my lungs. When I finally surfaced gasping for air, my lungs wouldn't work properly. I feared that the next breath would not come. I have never wanted to breathe so badly in my entire life.

The desire for faith is similar. It is as instinctual as our next breath. Most of the time, we take our next breath for granted. Likewise, we take our natural faith for granted and are often unaware of that faith until something threatens it. In order for our natural faith to grow and to evolve, we must accept that it is an innate gift given to us at our conception. We did not have to earn it, and it can't be taken from us unless we choose to give it away. It is part of the "hardware" of our divine computer. We may develop certain beliefs about how to tap into this faith, and we may even wonder whether we deserve it. Our natural faith may also be stretched to its limits by the disappointments we face in life. But it is always available to use. Indeed, it is essential to our existence.

Like flowers seeking sunshine, we are attracted to those things that nourish us. Natural faith both nourishes and motivates us. It is the driving force behind our belief—childlike, but not childish—that our lives always unfold toward the good. Such faith, like a divine potion, allows us to overcome seemingly insurmountable challenges. Most important, it opens us to *God's* infinite goodness.

FAITH ENHANCER

In your journal, write a statement that describes your commitment to your natural faith. Make an agreement with yourself that you will not surrender this faith to anyone or anything.

God as a Person

When my granddaughter was ten years old, I baby-sat her one afternoon. She is an alert and curious child, and for the entire afternoon, I fielded a barrage of questions about every event we encountered. She asked me why lizards do push-ups. She asked me why some clouds are darker than others. She asked me if I liked having less hair than her grandma did. Many questions had no factual answers, so I made them up. It became a game—her curiosity versus my imagination. I managed an answer to every question. Later that night, I fell exhausted into bed. Since that fateful day, my granddaughter has had an unending faith in me. She thinks I hung the moon. For her, I am one of those endless "givers" who is bigger than life—one of those people you can always count on. So far, I have managed not to disappoint her.

Our connection to our faith and to our God is similar. The divine gift of faith places us in relationship with a powerful "giver"—a relationship similar to the one we have with our parents when we are children, or the one that we as grandparents, have with our grandchildren. As we mature, it is natural to view our "giving" God as a person, one from whom we yearn for answers about the circumstances and challenges in our lives. Our natural faith grows stronger and more tenacious, and our search for answers to our problems can produce miraculous results.

Such was the story of my parents' departure from Cuba. In 1960, one year after Castro's revolution, my mother decided that our family would immigrate to the United States. The government had closed the parochial schools where the children had been educated, and my father had lost most of his business. Against mounting odds, she managed to smuggle all four children into the United States. She and my father, who was recovering from an illness, remained behind. Soon after her children left, my mother began arranging for their departure, too. This required permission from the Cuban government, a U.S. visa and a mode of transportation. At the time, there were thousands of people trying to leave Cuba. Consequently, the waiting lines at the various government offices were days long. My mother would often spend the night in line so that she would not lose her place. More often than not, when she arrived at the front of a line, she would be turned away. The immigration process seemed interminable, but her faith drove her on.

My mother's natural faith was unending. She was never one for religious dogma and ecclesiastical rules, and her close friends often criticized her for not following the letter of the catechism. Her response was always the same: "If I do everything that the mother church wants me to do, I will lose my faith." Now that statement comes from a mature faith! Buoyed by that faith, my mother was so convinced that they would soon get out of the country that she moved out of her house and into a hotel with my convalescing father. There she waited further news about their departure.

Once she received word that their visas were imminent, she desperately began trying to find a mode of transportation. The wait for airline passage was months long, and my parents' visas would expire by the time their reservations could be validated. Frantic, my mother asked for help from a priest who was related to the owner of a boat that ferried people back and forth to Florida. The priest referred her for an interview with the owner, who was gracious but assured her that reservations on the boat were impossible. Nevertheless, the day she actually received the visas, she again appeared at the boat owner's door, begging him to allow them passage. This time the owner was firm. He waved her away, emphasizing that the boat would leave the following Monday for the last time and that there was absolutely no room left.

That visit occurred on a Friday afternoon. My mother returned to the hotel and shared the story with my father, but optimistically reassured him that they would find a way. She never stopped her prayers.

On Sunday, she insisted that they go to a church service that they had never attended before. During the service, she noticed that the boat owner was present. When the service was over, she started to approach him. My father was vehemently opposed to this. "You will only embarrass yourself," he said. But my mother insisted, explaining that she only wanted to thank the boat owner for listening to her and attempting to help. When she approached him, the boat owner became wide-eyed. As she began to express her gratitude, he interrupted her saying, "Mrs. Monserrat, we have been trying to find you all weekend. We have had two cancellations and have saved the space for you! Please be at the dock early tomorrow morning." Stunned and in shock, my mother began to walk away. The boat owner followed her. He tapped her on the shoulder and asked, "Mrs. Monserrat, have you and your husband ever attended this church before?" My mother said, "No, we never have." Dazed and amazed he said, "Neither have I."

My mother had a vision that she would be reunited with her entire family. She tells me now that she remained in constant prayer throughout that ordeal. Though there was only a slight chance of their leaving Cuba, she remained optimistic through her faith. In the end, it was her faith and her relationship with God that made the miracle happen.

FAITH ENHANCERS

Take a moment to write the history of your God. Start with your earliest impressions and memories about God. Who first taught you about the concept of the divine, and how was that concept refined through religious education? Was there one particular time or incident that redefined God for you? Did you have any miraculous experiences that boosted your concept of God to new heights?

A Life of Expectations

My mother's faith is natural. Although she also depends on her religion, she mostly relies on her natural faith. When our faith is in its natural state, we expect our lives to unfold in specific ways. In fact, we bank our faith on it. At this faith level, our relationship with God is one of dependency, and our prayers become a kind of pleading—we describe our expectations and expect particular outcomes. We believe that if all else fails, we can turn to prayer. Of course, there is also the occasional "Thank God!" when a specific expectation is met.

For several years I worked with a woman who was unable to maintain an intimate relationship, although that was something she very much wanted. Instead, she tumbled from one relationship to the next, rationalizing each separation. There was always something wrong with the prospective partner, and she had specific expectations that were somehow never met. She viewed successful relationships as a matter of chance and therefore believed she had to go through many of them until the right relationship came along.

She was raised in a traditional religion that her parents participated in only because "it was good for appearances." Her relationship with God, whom she viewed as a domineering male figure, was filled with distrust. Her early attempts at intimacy with older men left her disappointed and unsatisfied. Her marriage ended with her husband abandoning her and inflicting a deep wound on her capacity to trust. Since then, she had been in and out of depression. Her faith was vulnerable, and she lost it often.

The initial phase of the work was to have her learn to trust me. Our relationship remained delicate for many months, and my posture was mostly supportive and agreeable. She needed a male figure who was authoritative and who accepted her unconditionally. As her trust in me developed, she started to follow my guarded advice. She started practicing meditation and sacred dance. She went back to school and completed an advanced degree in counseling. Most important, she stopped rushing into relationships and became more cautious about her choices.

Although this woman had resigned herself to a life of hit-and-miss affairs, during our work she was able to strengthen her natural faith—and thus increase her chances of having a healthy relationship. I encouraged her to stop pleading with her God, whom she didn't trust anyway, and begin using affirmative prayer. "It is time you got yourself a new God," I told her. "Your old one is not serving you well." As her faith matured, this woman came to trust herself. Her expectations about the kind of man and relationship that she wanted became more clear and concise. Several years later, I encountered her with a companion. She reported having been with him for some time.

FAITH ENHANCERS

Set aside time to write down several goals for yourself. (Instead of writing, you may choose to sketch, paint or decoupage.) These goals should be something you can observe and measure. Describe your desires and expectations around each goal; be as detailed and specific as possible. Now go to your daily or yearly planner and set up a timeline for accomplishing each goal. Spend time each day working toward your goals and affirming positive outcomes.

Toward a New Version of God

Our natural faith tells us that the goodness of life is mere chance, and that our prayers are *probably* heard and answered. The results of our praying depend mostly on the mood of the almighty person we call God. We spend a great deal of time hoping that things will turn out okay. Eventually we become resigned to a life of chance and unpredictability.

So it was with me. Not unlike the client I just discussed, I, too, had grown up in a traditional religion that emphasized an authoritative God. My God was volatile, and his whimsical moods were impossible to guess. My God also played favorites—in our religion, we believed that we were "saved," while people of other beliefs were damned. By the time I was nineteen, I had had enough of that religion.

Along with discarding my religion, I got rid of my early concept of God. I embarked on a journey that was devoid of any God. It was a lonely and depressing journey, and I experienced a "dark night of the soul" that went on for several years. In retrospect, I see that period as a total cleansing of an old belief system that had been deeply ingrained in my mind and my heart. It would be almost three years before I embraced a new version of God. It happened after I had returned to the United States from a Peace Corps tour in Central America. I had started a meditation practice, begun studying Eastern religions and changed many of my living habits. I had also started my postgraduate work in counseling psychology, and the course work for one of our classes took me on a retreat to Abiquiu in northern New Mexico. The landscape there is magical and for years has attracted famous artists for its inspirational powers. The setting worked its magic on me, too.

The focus of the retreat was to search for the true values in our lives. After a particularly intense session, I went for a hike to a rock outcropping which overlooked a valley 100 miles long. During the entire walk I felt restless. Though I had learned much about God in the previous year, I sensed that my search was not complete. I began to talk aloud. There was frustration in my voice. "Okay, God. If you exist, I need you to show up now," I shouted repeatedly. Finally, as I reached the top of the rock and looked at the mesmerizing landscape, a shift in my thinking occurred. I realized that my dialogue with God was but a conversation with some aspect of me. At that moment, not only was my definition of God transformed, but also my definition of self. From this epiphany grew a new relationship with my higher power. The divine was no longer an anthropomorphic, authoritative God. Instead, this new divinity was a very personal and inner being. This God was inside me!

The story of my epiphany is the story of my rebirth. During the dark time when I had disconnected with my higher power, I lost my childhood religion and God. Although the trauma of those losses distanced me from my higher power, there was still a yearning within me that led me to continue my spiritual search. A deep sense of hope had always stayed with me. This is the hope that comes with our natural faith. No matter how long we may stay away from God, religion or prayer, the hopeful craving for the goodness of life remains.

In the Evolution of Faith matrix, hope is the essential emotional response of natural faith. We all have it, and if given half a chance, it will emerge. As it does, so does a new relationship with our higher power. This new relationship often grows out of desperate situations that humble us. Humbled, we are forced to shed our old skins to make room for new versions of God, ourselves and of life. Our new God then instills a new faith—and we best be prepared!

FAITH ENHANCER

Write a letter to your higher power. Tell the divinity who and what you think God is and what you hope to obtain from your relationship.

The Power of Pleading Our Case

When we feel desperate, we have an instinctive urge to plead to our higher power to intervene on our behalf. This is primal prayer. We search for something that we believe is outside of us. Eventually, we may have a fateful encounter that shakes up our old ways of believing. We then begin a new phase in the evolution of our faith. This often happens in unforeseen ways.

Let me tell you a story. Years ago, when we were young and naive, my wife and I went on a three-day rafting trip. We chose to navigate the Rio Grande river in northern New Mexico through particularly treacherous terrain. I had previously backpacked into the region and was somewhat familiar with it. In this high desert area, drinking water is not easy to find. Nevertheless, I thought that I could detect a canyon that had a small stream which would satisfy our thirst.

Late in the afternoon of our second day, we ran out of drinking water. We were tired and thirsty. On the toxic and polluted river, the temperature was more than 100 degrees, with little or no breeze moving through the canyon. We touched land at the entrance of a particularly deep canyon that I was sure was the one with a stream flowing through it. We left the raft on a sandy beach at the mouth of the canyon and began to hike in.

The heat of the afternoon sun was merciless. With no water to drink, every mile up the canyon felt like a walk into Hades. Tired and dehydrated, I began to plead aloud. "Okay, God. Where is the water?" I yelled. No more than a minute after my fit, we heard a rumble high above the cliff walls. Thunder. A mammoth thunderstorm appeared overhead, and it began to hail. Then rain came flooding down in epic proportions. "A flash flood," I yelled to Catherine, starting to run down the canyon. After a full three-mile sprint, we were able to reach the raft just before a wall of water, mud and debris would have pushed it into the river and left us stranded in the wilderness.

I have sometimes kidded about the effectiveness of that pleading prayer. God responds to a desperate request, but not always the way we expect. If I had listened to my intuition, I never would have gone up that canyon. Instead, I would have built a fire, boiled the water from the river and spared us much hardship. As we will learn later, mature prayer is the art of listening to and speaking with the divine and recognizing guidance when it comes. But for the moment, let us recognize that pleading is a natural, automatic response to our desperate needs.

Natural faith encourages hopefulness. We believe that we have a good chance for a better life and we form expectations based on that belief. Then we simply wait for the right outcomes. Unfortunately, we also resign ourselves to those outcomes, or we use pleading prayer to an authoritative deity to intervene on our behalf. These prayers may or may not be answered as our expectations dictate. If we don't receive answers, and our disappointment is too great, we may even experience a loss of faith.

FAITH ENHANCER

Make a list of the experiences that "steal" your faith. Make a note of any patterns that recur. These patterns are the manifestations of your hidden beliefs.

Restoring Our Natural Faith

Our natural faith may be lost for brief or extended periods that may vary in emotional intensity depending on many factors. These include our physical and mental health, our childhood upbringing, our religious training, our personal relationship to our higher power and finally, what people call our "personality." This last factor, though observable, is unexplainable. Some people seem to be born with an optimistic attitude that sustains them through a great deal of trauma and disappointment. For the rest of us, such optimistic faith is an ongoing quest.

Our natural faith may be restored in a variety of ways. Some of these are inherent healing qualities and may include something as simple as having a deep cry, a good, angry fit, confiding in a friend, walking in nature, reading an inspirational story or simply focusing our attention in the present moment. This last one includes noticing our feelings and our reactions in the moment, too.

A few years ago, my father was dying. I was living in Seattle at the time and was not able to be with him. My grief was deep. Pain oozed from parts of me that I did not know existed. It became difficult to get through the day, and all aspects of my faith were affected. When the pain became intolerable, I would go for a walk. I made an agreement with myself that I would not return until I found peace. I took long walks along the waterfront. Nature has a healing quality of its own, and I used it fully.

As my father's dying process continued, it was difficult to tell when I should go home to be with him. I was in daily contact with my siblings who, along with my mother, were helping me figure out what to do. I wanted to be with him at the time of his death, but I could not afford to go and then return for his funeral. Every other day I received a telephone call urging me to come, only to be followed by another call asking me to wait. Making a decision became excruciating. During one of my long walks, the answer was revealed. I would stop listening to my family and trust my own intuition. I knew that the only way to access that intuition was by staying in the moment. A few days later, again on one of my walks, the need to be with my father overwhelmed me. I booked the next flight and arrived in time to speak to him. He died the following day.

There is a wealth of wisdom and strength to be culled from staying in the present. This is sacred time. Practicing being "in the moment," together with praying, can help restore our natural faith. When we rely on that faith, we no longer have to worry about the decisions we make, or the outcomes of those decisions. We will know that a higher wisdom is at play in our lives, and only good will prevail.

CHAPTER THREE

When Faith Is Lost

We are wiser than we know.
If we will not interfere with our thought,
but will act entirely, or see how the thing stands
in God, we know the particular thing, and every man.
For the Maker of all things and all persons stands
behind us and casts his dread omniscience
through us over things.

—*Ralph Waldo Emerson*

Not all guidance is as clear as what I received when my father was dying, nor is every expectation met the way we want it to be. Often we must navigate our lives through periods that not only resemble my own "dark night of the soul," but which are also down and dirty blackouts. Such episodes deplete our faith. They extract a "pound of flesh" from our spiritual bodies and rob us of our natural buoyancy. We lose our natural faith when we turn fearful thoughts into hardened beliefs, or we experience traumatic events that convince us our lives are unsafe and unpredictable.

The Effects of Trauma on the Mind

Several years ago, an elderly woman came to see me. I guessed that she was in her eighties. She had listened to several of my Sunday lectures and was taken by what I had to say. She said that she had been searching for her faith in God for many years but had not managed to find it. She had plenty of faith in herself and had handled her life well. Now that she was getting older, however, her faith seemed insufficient.

She spoke in a slow and deliberate manner, and there was a great deal of pain in her eyes. I asked her to tell me about her life. The wrinkles that covered her face already told a powerful story. *This is not an ordinary woman,* I thought. I allowed her to tell her story over a period of months. She said that as a young child she had had to hide a physical defect that kept her from playing sports. Her family had been very poor, and her mother was forced to work. Her father had been in frail health and unavailable to her. Through hard work, she had put herself through college and earned a teaching degree.

She married soon after graduation and settled into caring for her household and her three children. The youngest child was sickly and became seriously ill. Her family physician prescribed some medication, which she administered, but her child had a catastrophic reaction to it and died. The young mother blamed herself for the horrible mistake. To make matters worse, while the family was still grieving, her husband took their oldest son to the park to ignite a rocket they had built. The rocket misfired, killing the father and maiming the son. The young woman now found herself alone with two children, one of them disabled, and she needed to work to support them. In a matter of weeks, she found a job teaching. There was no time to grieve.

She carried her guilt and pain for years. She endured her life through sheer determination, which she had learned from her parents. She worked hard and managed her family the best that she could. Now that she was elderly, however, her hope and optimism were gone. Her faith in God was lost. I encouraged her to trust being in the moment and to really feel her despair. This was challenging, since she had hid her wounds for many decades. She did not completely trust the process. In time, however, she gave into the emotions behind her stories, which I had her repeatedly tell me. We would pray at the end of each session. I told her that she no longer needed the God who had allowed all those things to happen to her. I encouraged her instead to pursue the God inside her—a God who would give her courage and vision.

Slowly her dark mood began to lift. She became a regular at our Sunday services. I asked her what her vision for the rest of her life was. This puzzled her, since she had come to accept her death as imminent. I asked her to do some spiritual homework—to write down what she would like to accomplish before her death—and she dutifully took on the task. She managed to stop blaming herself for her son's death, and she chose to spend some delicious time with her second husband. She learned to embrace joy. After a year, she became a "light" in the congregation. People would comment on her demeanor and disposition. Although her age was starting to take its toll, she was cheerful and friendly. We would speak from time to time over the next several years, and would always joke about that deep period of despair that we spent together talking. She died peacefully surrounded by her family.

Life deals each of us some difficult cards to play from time to time. It is impossible to say why. The above story happens to be one of the most traumatic histories that I have encountered in my professional life. I am sure, though, that there are other stories that are even more devastating. There is an old saying that goes: "God does not give us any more than we can handle." This can certainly be true, but it doesn't mean that we will not lose our faith while we're trying to handle what comes our way.

It is important to note the symptoms that accompany lost faith. In the above story, the woman lived in constant fear and despair. These are emotional signs of eroding faith. We may also find ourselves blaming others—or ourselves—for unexpected outcomes or problems for which no one is to blame. When faith is lost, we may also be angry and feel a need to express it—in fact, we may find ourselves uttering curses rather than saying prayers. If the loss of faith is chronic, we may feel hopeless and cynical and have a tendency to fall into frequent depressions.

FAITH ENHANCER

Set aside some time to think about a traumatic event in your life. Write your story down or speak it into a tape recorder. Give yourself permission and time to reexperience all the emotions around that trauma. You may be surprised by the feelings that surface. Consider sharing your story with a close friend, therapist or spiritual advisor.

A Life of Victimization

Trauma can have a deep impact on an individual's personality. I have encountered several people whose chronic trauma has carved deep grooves of despair into their personalities; often, they choose to live life as victims. Their loss of faith frequently begins in childhood with cynical and distrustful parents who don't expect much goodness from life. Such parents often demand too much from their children, and whenever anything goes wrong, the children are blamed. There is constant tension in the household, and substance abuse or alcoholism is often a problem. Child abuse is also common and can be physical or emotional.

Such children grow up without much self-confidence and faith. They seem destined for a life of victimization. Indeed, victimization can become a self-fulfilling prophecy. When these children are adults, they often choose abusive relationships and/or work situations. In a desperate need for praise, such individuals may remain

READER/CUSTOMER CARE SURVEY

We care about your opinions. Please take a moment to fill out this Reader Survey card and mail it back to us.
As a special **"thank you"** we'll send you exciting news about interesting books and a valuable **Gift Certificate.**

Please PRINT using ALL CAPS

First Name ____________ MI. __ Last Name ____________

Address ____________

City ____________ ST ____ Zip ______ – ______

Phone # (____) ____ – ______ Fax # (____) ____ – ______

Email ____________

(1) Gender:

______Female ______Male

(2) Age:

______12 or under ______40-59
______13-19 ______60+
______20-39

(3) Marital Status

______Married
______Single
______Divorced/Widowed

(4) Did you receive this book as a gift?

______Yes ______No

(5) How many Health Communications books have you bought or read?

______1 ______2-4 ______5+

(6) How did you find out about this book?
Please fill in ***ONE.***

1)______Recommendation
2)______Store Display
3)______Bestseller List
4)______Online
5)______Advertisement
6)______Catalog/Mailing
7)______Interview/Review (TV, Radio, Print)

(7) Where do you usually buy books?
Please fill in your top ***TWO*** *choices.*

1)______Bookstore
2)______Religious Bookstore
3)______Online
4)______Book Club/Mail Order
5)______Price Club (Costco, Sam's Club, etc.)
6)______Retail Store (Target, Wal-Mart, etc.)

(9) What subjects do you enjoy reading about most? Rank only ***FIVE.*** *Use 1 for your favorite, 2 for second favorite, etc.*

	1	2	3	4	5
1) Parenting/Family	O	O	O	O	O
2) Relationships	O	O	O	O	O
3) Recovery/Addictions	O	O	O	O	O
4) Health/Nutrition	O	O	O	O	O
5) Christianity	O	O	O	O	O
6) Spirituality/Inspiration	O	O	O	O	O
7) Business Self-Help	O	O	O	O	O
8) Teen Issues	O	O	O	O	O
9) Sports	O	O	O	O	O

(14) What attracts you most to a book?
(Please rank 1-4 in order of preference.)

	1	2	3	4
1) Title	O	O	O	O
2) Cover Design	O	O	O	O
3) Author	O	O	O	O
4) Content	O	O	O	O

TAPE IN MIDDLE; DO NOT STAPLE

BUSINESS REPLY MAIL

FIRST-CLASS MAIL PERMIT NO 45 DEERFIELD BEACH, FL

POSTAGE WILL BE PAID BY ADDRESSEE

HEALTH COMMUNICATIONS, INC.
3201 SW 15TH STREET
DEERFIELD BEACH FL 33442-9875

FOLD HERE

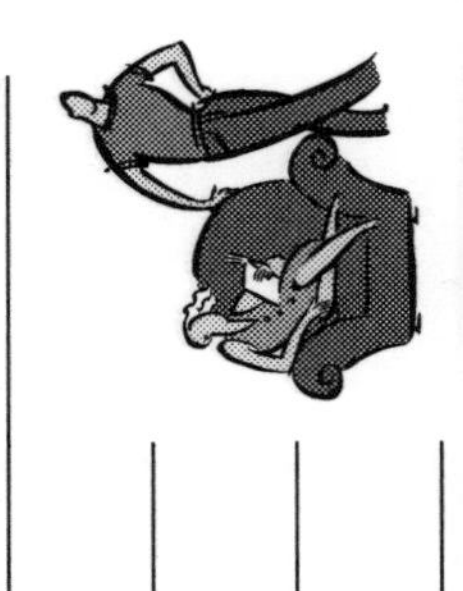

Comments:

in abusive situations long after these have stopped functioning well. When they eventually fail in a relationship or on a job, some people feel further victimized and go on to live a life of little or no faith. Their God tends to be but a fleeting thought that has no real definition. They live their lives with little insight into who they really are and what they are capable of being. Their doubts about themselves are projected onto the world and onto God. Their self-esteem is so low that they are usually incapable of taking responsibility for their behavior. Eventually, they fall into a pit of darkness where the future is nothing but a void.

Our childhood histories often hide the key to the vault where our natural faith is stored away. For many of us our natural faith is not only hidden, it is also lost in our subconscious memories. Our childhood may have been so painful that we have mental lags and memory loss. This is often the case with severe physical or sexual abuse. As abused children, we may cope with early trauma by dissociating ourselves from the memories—and, sadly, from the natural faith with which we were born. When we are adults, our lives often become a constant struggle to reclaim that faith. (I will have more to say about regaining our faith in chapter 4.)

FAITH ENHANCER

Draw a childhood lifeline. Do this by drawing a horizontal line across a piece of paper. On the left end of the line, write down your birth date. On the right end of the line, write down the age when you became independent (or left home). Starting with your earliest memories, draw a second, curvy line graphing the "high" and the "low" points of your childhood. High points are drawn above your lifeline; low points appear below your lifeline. The happier the event (e.g., a special birthday party, a new puppy), the higher the curve; likewise, the more traumatic the event (e.g., a move to a new home, parents' divorce), the lower the curve. The graph to follow will give you an example of an honest view of your childhood. You will be able to compare the highs and lows, how long they lasted and how significant they were. You may want to speak with your parents about the periods you don't remember well.

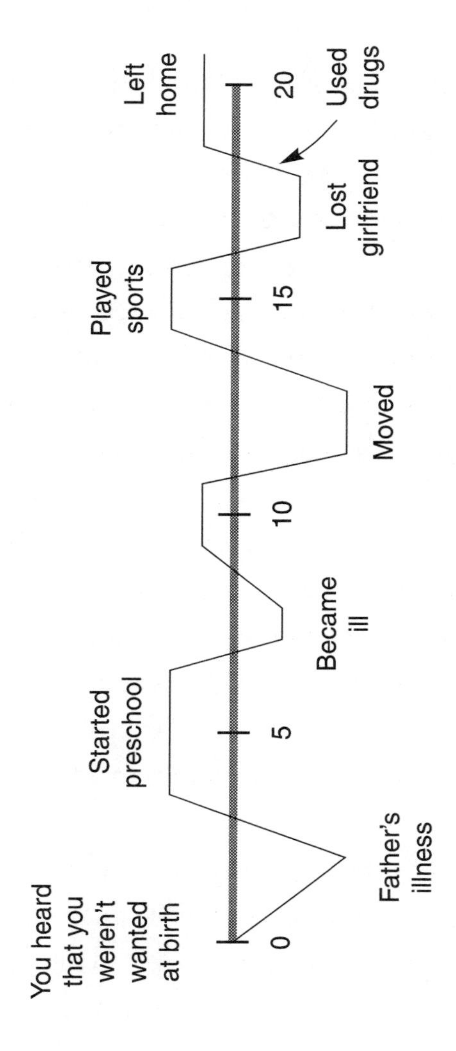
You heard that you weren't wanted at birth
Father's illness
Started preschool
Became ill
Moved
Played sports
Lost girlfriend
Used drugs
Left home
0
5
10
15
20

Darkness and Paralysis

The most intrusive aspect of the loss of faith is the way it darkens our spirit and "paralyzes" our lives. Our spirit darkens because we are unable to access God. When our faith is lost, so is our intimacy with a higher power that can restore our well-being. Our hearts close and our minds shut down. We become focused on the improbability and imperfections of our life. Then paralysis sets in. The paralysis of lost faith may act like quick-setting cement, bringing all our hopeful actions to a halt. Or it may feel like quicksand, slowly bringing us to a state of helplessness, even as we struggle to get free. Denying our condition makes it worse and prevents us from seeking help. Soon we either become accustomed to our dark, immobilized state, or we isolate ourselves, making help and change even more difficult. But we must always remember that our capacity to change our situations and ourselves is infinite.

A few Christmases ago, my wife, Catherine, vowed that she would not spend another holiday with me. She threatened to fly to Hawaii by herself. The threat should not have caught me by surprise. For as long as I could remember, the holiday season had been difficult for me. Nevertheless, I would usually "muscle" my way through it. My somber moods made her miserable. Unable to avoid her discomfort any longer, I had to confront my feelings about the holiday. I tried to remember the last Christmas I had enjoyed. My self-examination took me back to the Christmas—over thirty years ago—when I was told that I would be leaving my family and immigrating to the United States without my parents. My childhood dream of family was shattered. I buried my anger, and my only tool for coping was to reject the Christmas holiday.

Once I had overcome my original (and continued) denial, I was open to solutions. I placed myself on a "spiritual diet" of affirmations and positive prayer. My prayers were soon answered. I found the courage to seek professional help, and that had positive results. My natural faith was restored, and so was my good mood during the holidays. I was no longer at the mercy of my moods, and neither was Catherine!

FAITH ENHANCER

Make a list of the situations that challenge you or paralyze you—e.g., confronting your partner, investing money, starting an exercise program, going back to school, dating, looking for employment, completing projects, being aware of seasonal mood swings. Contemplate your list; consider your feelings and actions around those situations, then try to observe any denial patterns that you practice. How can you break a particular pattern of denial?

Ignorance and the Return to Light

Our spiritual ignorance is not related to our intelligence, but rather to our wisdom. Our darkness persists because we become used to it, not because we can't figure out how to turn on the light. We become resigned to it. In our resignation, we fail to exercise our divine gift of choice, and thus more paralysis sets it. When my wife put her foot down and refused to put up with my dark holiday moods, I had to confront my ignorance. My denial about what had happened to me as a child had kept me stuck in a certain mind-set. With some self-analysis and prayer, I was able to touch my childhood pain and release it. I built a support system that allowed me to tell my story. I also explored some remedies that were helpful. In time, some light crept into the holiday darkness.

I have come to trust in the goodness of life. I also try not to fool myself. I know that I have monsters in my closet. I am working hard to know them and "befriend" them. The more I do that, the more I recognize my monsters for what they are. Whenever I face one, I get stronger and my faith increases. I am coming to accept one of my teacher's assertions: "Life is rigged for success."

It also helps to stay focused on the bottom line. Most painful events in life are not life threatening—we usually make them so. We often face our Goliaths as if they were out to annihilate us. Usually, they are just there to help us rustle up some courage and sharpen our spiritual aims. There is a story about David talking to one of his generals shortly after defeating Goliath. The general asks David, "How did you do that?" David answers, "How could I not? With a target so big, I couldn't miss!"

FAITH ENHANCER

Write yourself a letter and give yourself a pep talk. Make it a rousing, old-fashioned, "that-a-boy" or "that-a-girl" testament to your greatness. Think of all your positive qualities, and make sure you include your capacity to learn.

Do this in front of a mirror. Make eye contact with yourself often.

CHAPTER FOUR

Regaining Our Faith

Do not be timid and squeamish about your actions. All life is an experiment. The more experiments you make the better. What if they are a little coarse, and you may get your coat soiled or torn? What if you do fail, and get fairly rolled in the dirt once or twice? Up again you shall never be so afraid of a tumble.

—*Ralph Waldo Emerson*

The first step toward regaining our faith is to recognize that we are in trouble and need help. Help comes in a variety of ways and from many sources. We can start by accepting the messages that our body and mind send us—they never lie. For example, if we are in pain or are engaging in addictive behavior, our body and mind are probably telling us that we had better do something about our faith.

The quality of our relationships is another way of gauging faith. If we are isolating from others—our spouse, close friends or society in general—it's time to evaluate our level of faith. If we are losing interest in our work, failing to commit ourselves to certain tasks or constantly wishing that we were some place else, a loss of faith may be part of the problem.

Asking for Help

The first step in regaining our faith—once we have accepted that it is lost or weakened—is reaching out for help. Of course, we prize our independence: Asking for help is no easy task. We might first reach out to our spouse, significant other or a longtime friend. Whoever we choose, it should be someone who knows us and is not afraid to give us his or her opinion. By the time you notice that something is wrong, it's a good bet others have noticed, too. Support groups are also places to reach out for help. Many of us are involved in men's or women's groups or Twelve-Step programs that are based on spiritual principles. One-on-one spiritual counseling with a professional is also useful. As a minister, I am, of course, on the front line of this issue. I am often the first or second person to be contacted by a distressed individual. It is my job to help such people identify their level of misery and assess how their lives are being affected by a lack of faith.

Years ago a young woman called me long distance. She had been a visitor at our church and had since been receiving and listening to my Sunday lecture tapes. She was unhappy with her job, where she had worked for a dozen years. I asked her some questions about the job and sensed that it really wasn't the issue. I then asked her about other aspects of her life. I soon learned that she was dissatisfied with her marriage and confused about how to make things better. She was married to a wonderful, loving man who adored her. They were best friends, and since neither had any siblings, they were also each other's family. This woman cherished her friendship with her husband, but wanted a different kind of intimate relationship with a man. Her distress was understandable: She believed that if she left her husband she would lose her best friend and be all alone.

We began to do a lot of prayer work. I gave her specific issues to pray about regarding her sense of "aloneness." Our work was slow and tedious, but in time she was able to acknowledge her lack of faith in herself and in her childhood God. We also unraveled the childhood history that had triggered her difficulties in intimate relationships. Her mother had died when she was a child, at a time when she was just starting to develop her sense of identity. She had to rely on her father, an ex-marine sergeant who was emotionally unavailable to her. Her self-esteem was shaky, and she was afraid of being rejected by the boys she found truly attractive. This woman dated only boys whom she liked as friends, but not as potential lovers.

I encouraged her to build a support system that included friends, prayer partners and support groups. She began practicing daily prayer, yoga and meditation. Her relationship with God improved, and she learned that she was never alone as long as she remembered she was in God's company. In time it became clear what needed to be done about her marriage. Through the process of strengthening her faith, she was able to dissolve the marriage but retain the friendship and sense of family with her ex-husband that she had most appreciated.

Life tends to unravel at the fragile edges of our relationship with God—those places in our emotional and/or spiritual makeup that are especially vulnerable. Where we have failed to build a strong connection with God, our lives are often tested and may even come undone. As mentioned earlier, our strongest beliefs about faith and God are often generated during the most difficult times of our lives. As in the case above, the death of a parent is a highly significant event—at any age. If that loss comes when we are children, and the support systems in our lives are unpredictable or unavailable to us, our trust in God will be affected. We may develop harsh beliefs about life and God that can last a lifetime. These beliefs will rule our lives until we take a good look at them, reject them and develop new, healthier beliefs.

FAITH ENHANCER

Write a letter to your parents. Whether your parents are dead or alive, attempt to bring closure to your relationship with them. If a relationship with one parent was significantly different from the one you had with your other parent, write separate letters to each. Tell them what you liked and disliked about the manner in which they raised you. Tell them what things you appreciated. Try to bring yourself to a place of forgiveness and gratitude. If you can't, you may need some help from a therapist or spiritual coach.

A Lifestyle of Faith Building

I recommend that everyone build support systems into their lives. These are safe environments where you can be yourself. They can be therapeutic groups, led by a professional, or simple get-togethers with a few friends who meet on a regular basis. What is important in such a group is that everyone can be open and honest. Confidentiality, of course, is essential. There is healing in "spilling our emotional guts," if for no other reason than the sheer relief of watching others help us pick them up! Our faith gets a boost when we learn that we are not the only ones in pain. Misery *does* love company, but it also hates to let go! So make sure your support system is emotionally healthy enough to deal with whatever comes up in group.

Other supports may include good friends, prayer groups, a therapist, a spiritual coach, spiritual retreats, medication (for depression/anxiety, if necessary), stress-reduction techniques, reading self-help and inspirational books, and walking in nature. Remember: a loss of faith can happen to any of us at any time. Major changes in our lives—and thus in our beliefs—may occur seemingly overnight. Some of the life changes that will shake our faith are: loss of a child, either to death or relocation;

dissolution of a marriage; loss of employment; relocation, thus losing immediate support systems; loss of health; loss of financial security. If you experience one or more of these at any particular time, you best know that you are susceptible to emotional trauma, thus an erosion of faith. If one of those changes catches us unprepared, spiritual darkness and paralysis can set in quickly. A good support system can go a long way to getting us on our "spiritual feet" again.

For years I promised myself to get some personal coaching about my managerial and organizational skills. But I had postponed doing so for many "good" reasons: "The budget will not allow it." "Whom can I trust?" "What will I talk about?" "Perhaps I don't really *need* it!" I kept putting the decision off. Then the church entered a difficult period, and I started to question my ministry there. I found myself getting angry at the slightest annoyance. When the finances started to fail, I knew I was in trouble. On a succession of Sundays, I noticed the attendance of a person who I knew was a business consultant. A few days later I called her and asked for her help.

I was not sure what to expect. I thought she would review the church's administrative structure, balance sheet, organizational chart, etc.—and then make some recommendations. It would all be easy and my frustrations would end. Was I wrong! What she required was that I make a six-month commitment to some personal coaching—the very thing I had been secretly seeking but afraid of manifesting! She had me look deeply at all my desires, expectations, goals and objectives. In our weekly meetings, we would examine each area of my ministry that was failing, or each goal that remained unaccomplished. She explored what my vision was for the church, the nature of my ministry, and each circumstance or person who was frustrating me.

My coach reminded me that manifestations start with God working through our visions. *Vision is the mental activity of our natural faith.* Results are attained when we firmly focus on the vision and declare a willingness to remove whatever obstacles get in its way. Without a conscious connection between our vision and our actions, we work against ourselves and our faith declines. Also vitally important to a lifestyle of faith building is the development of close relationships. Intimacy with one or several individuals is most helpful in maintaining our faith. Allowing someone to know us well, coming to trust their perceptions and learning to lean on their advice is a sure way to circumvent the paralysis of lost faith. These individuals have the potential to give us the information we need to break our denial. This is how my personal coach worked with me for many months. Ultimately, my faith in my ministry returned.

FAITH ENHANCER

Consider the following questions and write down your answers in your journal. What sustains your faith in yourself, in life and in God? Are you doing it alone? If so, who might help you? Are you willing to ask one or more individuals to form a support group? What about reaching out to an existing group?

Developing a Faith Philosophy

Being optimistic helps build strong faith. I am not talking about the nebulous "positive thinking" that has been popular over the last two decades. I refer to a well-thought-out discipline that builds confidence through its expansive qualities. This would be a philosophy that teaches the workings of the conscious and unconscious mechanisms of the mind, and supports our ability to influence them. A philosophy that teaches a religious tool that, with practice, will help us take aim at life's proverbial shifts. This is the start of an educated faith. (I will discuss these concepts in depth in chapter 5.) Developing such a discipline helped me overcome my personal "Goliath"—writing. Indeed, this book is a good example of optimistic faith in action.

Writing has always been a formidable task for me. Back in first grade, in the high-ceilinged classroom of my Jesuit school in Cuba, calligraphy was a requirement. Before we could write letters (we were not allowed to print), however, we had to master the "tubes and sticks" of the Palmer method of penmanship. My writing looked like hieroglyphics. The best I ever managed was grooves on the desk from pressing too hard and chapped lips from an overstressed tongue. Furthermore, I did not learn English until I immigrated in the seventh grade. This has made me self-conscious about my ability to communicate both verbally and on paper. My congregation teases me about speaking in "Cubanisms," which are words and grammatical structures that flow from the mixture of the two languages. I laugh along with them, but that laughter hides a deep sense of inadequacy about my communication skills. This has caused me to approach writing with a mixture of eagerness and trepidation.

Unable to postpone this book any longer, I decided to try a new strategy. I went looking for the "pebble and slingshot" that would slay my personal Goliath of fear and self-doubt. I based my strategy on this philosophy: *There is an innate wisdom within me that I call God. This wisdom is constantly seeking to express itself creatively and lovingly. If anyone is going to do this writing, the divine will!* I call my divine wisdom God or higher power, and it is available to me at all times. I have learned to lean on it. If I can relax into the present moment, this wisdom flows into my consciousness. It has the power to alter old behaviors or habits, and influence the manner in which I perceive and interact with the world around me.

When I began to write this book, I scheduled a two-week sabbatical for myself—and took along my laptop computer. Before my hiatus, I went on a "spiritual diet" for three months. During that time, I practiced saying daily affirmations, such as "The divinity within me flows creatively through my writing." That targeted my natural creative process and activated my unconscious creative resources. I also asked my support groups to pray for me. The results were amazing. I was able to sit for hours at a time and write, although I am restless by nature. The writing flowed, and the right stories "appeared" just when I needed them.

I have come to know faith as the presence of God in my life. This divinity, in its wisdom and its love, is responsible for placing me here, and is available to me at all times through my intuition. God draws me to people and experiences through divine love. My belief in the way the divine works in my life bolsters my faith. It is ingrained in my consciousness. I need only give myself a simple reminder to bring that divinity into full expression.

FAITH ENHANCER

Set aside time to reflect on these questions. Write down your answers in your journal. What personal or spiritual philosophy supports my faith? What are my beliefs about the way that I am supported in my faith? When was the last time I "updated" my beliefs and my faith? Am I still practicing childhood beliefs? What are they and how do they affect my life?

Where Does Faith Go?

The title of this chapter, "Regaining Our Faith," is somewhat misleading. In actuality, our faith is never lost. It is impossible to lose our faith because it is a divine gift.

Faith remains with us always, even when we are blind to its presence or think it is lost. We may move through our lives as if we didn't have this gift, but in fact, we have a choice when it comes to faith. I call it the "beauty and the beast" option. Remember we have free will—we are able to freely choose who and what we want to be. This is God's greatest gift to us. If we opt to remain ignorant, we will be ignorant. This is the "beast." On the other hand, if we choose to embrace our natural, God-given faith, we will reap the great benefits of this unending gift. This is "beauty."

To awaken from our ignorance, we have two choices: We can either learn about the nature of our divine inheritance, or we can wait for the wake-up call. Being hit over the head—even metaphorically—by life's circumstances may involve some pain and staggering around a bit. Eventually, however, we usually come to our spiritual senses. *We come to believe that there is a higher power within us, and we can use that power to our benefit.* First and foremost this involves becoming humble in the face of our divine nature. Then we can build our "spiritual muscles" with regular spiritual practices and education that will sustain us through bouts of lost faith. When we have a regular spiritual practice, our "bouts of doubt" (as I call them) do not tend to last as long, nor are they as intense. Our spiritual muscles can be put to work at any time. Although we may experience some pain and discomfort from life's predicaments, we can recover more quickly from their effects.

The discipline of study, meditation and prayer is a lifelong program that must be practiced if one wishes to progress in the faith-building journey. Spiritual discipline is the mainstay of an educated faith. In order to shake off our "bouts of doubt" and our "lack attacks," we must exercise the spiritual muscles that are built through spiritual exercises. A complete faith-education program will include many components. In addition to the ones mentioned earlier—study, meditation and prayer—a faith-building regimen may also include: exercising daily; eating a balanced diet; developing intimacy with at least one person; caring for a person (group, pet, social cause, etc.); having a creative outlet (needlework, painting, sculpting, etc.); and practicing silence, solitude and simply doing nothing. What is most important is that we come to accept our faith education as a lifelong endeavor with some form of daily practice. Let me tell you a story.

I have held administrative positions for the past twenty years. This has required that I hire a fair number of employees. I have never liked the hiring process. Regardless of how careful the selection process, it always seems like a crapshoot. During my ministry at the church, I have hired several church managers with varying degrees of success. The last one was easy. She walked into my office, laid her qualifications and experience on my desk and cried until I gave her the position. She did a superb job for three years, and I had grown quite attached to her. Her departure and the prospect hiring a replacement upset me. Reading dozens of résumés, conducting interviews and making a final decision seemed more than I could manage at the time. I told the board of directors about my predicament, and they agreed to help. We formed a committee and divided the tasks. A clear winner emerged and we hired her. She lasted two months.

My faith was now shot. We had wasted time, money and energy. Worst of all, I was furious at everyone, including God. Then in one of my meditation sessions, I received an answer to my persistent prayer for the right person: "Let God choose this person." *Gee, what a novel idea,* I thought. I set an intention to allow God to choose this individual. For my part, I would continue to pray whenever I found myself anxious about the process. The results were immediate. Three members of the congregation requested the job. This confused me, but I remembered that my job was simply to pray. Whenever I remembered to pray, answers emerged. The divine within me said, "Wait until the right one presents herself." When two of the candidates decided to drop out of the running, the one left was the clear choice. She is still with me after a couple of years and doing an excellent job.

Though it seemed like my faith was lost, it had only gone into hiding. Disappointment can do this. It is only human that we run out of patience dealing with life's dilemmas. But these are precisely the times when we can boost our faith to the next level and build more spiritual muscle. These are the times for listening to our inner divine wisdom and learning to discern what is fear (on our part) and what is divine instruction. (Of course, this process isn't always easy. I have more to say about it in chapter 6, "Enlightened Faith.")

I have spoken of my "spiritual diets" and of setting intentions. These are two powerful tools for regaining our faith. One component of a spiritual diet is saying a specific prayer that focuses on a desired result. I recommend you say this prayer daily for at least six months. It usually takes that long to rework an old belief system. For example, I had inherited a frightening set of beliefs about money from my father. Regardless of our family's financial situation, he always believed we did not have enough money. I grew up with an entrenched belief in "lack." To break that belief pattern in my own life, I placed myself on a spiritual diet of specific prayers focused on having more money.

After about six months, more money started coming into my life. Then a most curious series of events occurred. I started losing money. I literally misplaced checks, overdrew my checking account and failed to enter checks into the register. I realized that for me, the issue was *not* about having more money, but about developing an "abundance consciousness." I simply was not ready to experience having more money until I learned to see myself as intrinsically prosperous. It was back to my spiritual diet. This time, however, I set an intention to recognize and embrace the abundance already in my life. I also prayed the following affirmation every day: *I live in an abundant universe. It is made by God, and thus it must reflect God's abundant nature.* Slowly, my attitudes about money and the way that it influences my life began to change. My "lack attacks" are rare today, and recently I noticed that I haven't asked Catherine to tighten the spending belt in some time!

Building spiritual muscles is the backbone of an educated faith. Not unlike our physical bodies, our faith bodies will strengthen through prayer diets and spiritual practices. You will be amazed how "miracles" start to appear in your life as you set an intention and make a commitment to building your faith. You can do this through any desire or need that currently challenges you. As an example, let's say that you desire (or even need) a long-term committed relationship. By either standing in front of a mirror, or in front of your best friend, declare your intention to seek such a relationship and make a commitment to this search. Place yourself on a spiritual diet of daily prayer and meditation. Last thing before falling asleep, and first thing upon waking, recite your affirmation. It could be something like: "I know that God wills me to be the perfect partner." During your meditation, listen to God's response. It may not always be what you expect or want to hear. For instance, the answer to your prayer may be: "Stop being so negative" or "Join the choir." You may find that God's answers will challenge your status quo, and require that you stretch your confidence in yourself and the world.

FAITH ENHANCER

Set an intention for a desired result in your life. Start with something small. Then compose an affirmative prayer that you will say last thing before falling to sleep and first thing upon waking. Commit to this practice for six months. Have patience, and give the Spirit within you a chance to work.

The Need for Coaching

Nobody said that we have to do this faith-building alone. In fact, we can't possibly have the right answer or take the right action for every troubling situation which confronts us. Often we may need what I call a "spiritual coach" to help us through specific dilemmas. God, who comes in all forms, is not only found within us, but also within the people around us. Indeed, God often helps us *through* a variety of people and events. A spiritual coach may be a close friend who shares our philosophical beliefs and is willing to be forthright and honest with us in giving advice. Consider using such a friend as a coach for less serious spiritual dilemmas, and remember to set specific guidelines for the coaching relationship so that your friendship isn't jeopardized.

You may want to consider hiring a professional coach for more serious spiritual problems. This individual can be a minister, priest, health practitioner, lay minister, professional mediator or a therapist. I recommend that any coach you choose have professional and spiritual training, and be adept at developing therapeutic, healing relationships. It is only within the context of such a relationship that you can honestly explore the obstacles to your faith. In time, a good coach will move you beyond the healing of your mental and spiritual wounds, and into the realm of your spiritual beliefs. You will then start to examine the beliefs that hinder your faith development. With skillful coaching, you will investigate the beliefs that hindered your faith building and spiritual growth. You may also have to confront—and change—behaviors that no longer work for you. Be patient, and remember that all struggles are grist for the spiritual mill!

In time, your coach will take a position of less importance in your life. Once you are well grounded in your spiritual philosophy, you will need less confrontation and teaching. After a while, you will simply "check in" with your coach to update him or her about your progress. There will be longer lags of time between coaching sessions, though it is important to keep your coach invested and involved. Let him or her know what's going on by telephone, letters, notes or e-mails. Occasionally, you may need to return to full-time coaching for a while. Follow your spiritual intuition.

FAITH ENHANCER

In your journal, describe the type of spiritual dilemma or crisis that you believe would benefit from spiritual coaching. Have you ever experienced such a dilemma or crisis? If so, did you heed the call for help? Why or why not?

Commit to Building Faith

Our capacity for faith is limited only by our history and the beliefs it created. The way we conceptualize our past influences our perceptions and subsequent choices. The more trauma and unresolved grief we carry, the more our natural tendency for hope and optimism decays. But every event in our lives is a faith-building opportunity. From the most victorious to the least significant, from the blissful to the painful, each life event is decreed by a higher wisdom and a deeper love. All experiences invite us to develop our faith. When we are willing to "lean" on God for spiritual insight and to trust in divine love, the troubling events of our lives will lead us to greater spiritual truths. We will then be able to fully partake of all God's bounty.

Make a commitment to build your faith. Declare your willingness to have every event in your life be a faith-building opportunity. Lean on the inner guidance that is your divine inheritance. By doing so, you will see the good not only in you, but also in those around you. And all will benefit.

FAITH ENHANCER

Select a single word—to say aloud or silently—that will remind you of your commitment to faith building. For some time now, my word has been "surrender." When accompanied by a couple of deep breaths, a word that is spoken with intention will produce miracles.

CHAPTER FIVE

An Educated Faith

We are all believers in natural religion; we all agree that the health and integrity of man is self-respect, self-subsistency, a regard to natural conscience. All education is to accustom him to trust himself, discriminate between his higher and lower thoughts, exert the timid faculties until they are robust, and thus train him to self-help, until he ceases to be an underling, a tool, and becomes a benefactor.

—Ralph Waldo Emerson

Not only have we been granted a natural faith, we have also been gifted with the capacity to learn. In fact, our potential for learning has been a major factor in the evolution of humankind. This evolution is most evident in science, but there is also an evolution of consciousness. The contributions that spiritual philosophy and psychology have made to this endeavor are astounding. Psychologists such as Carl Jung, Victor Frankl and William James, and spiritual philosophers such as Wayne Dyer, Ram Dass, Ernest Holmes, Deepak Chopra and Mary Manning Morrissey to name a few, have dug deep into the human psyche in order to learn about the evolutionary nature of the mind. Because of their work, we can educate ourselves about our faith, and in doing so, we can elevate our consciousness and enhance that faith.

Learning who we are is easy. Doing something about it often isn't. By the time we have the capacity to understand the psychological and spiritual components of our mind, our personal habits are well entrenched. We adapt our belief systems to our environments, and we are often caught in a cycle of repeating our history. We manage our crises of faith through sheer muscle and willpower and settle into a life of resignation.

If this pattern sounds familiar, do not despair. You can educate and increase your faith, but it will require commitment on your part, and a willingness to do whatever it takes to accomplish your goals. There is a wealth of spiritual material and paths available to assist you. In the end, however, the specific path you choose does not make a lot of difference. What is important is sticking to that path. You will eventually find a faith-building philosophy that will appeal to you.

I remember my early days of seeking. I was in my early twenties and was using mind-altering drugs that expanded my consciousness. I was enchanted with the results and in awe of what my mind could do. But these "trips" were short-lived. After a few hours I had to return to "normal" life. Then I heard of a psychologist from Harvard University named Richard Alpert. He and his cohorts had done a series of experiments with drugs that had revolutionized (and scandalized) the academic field. I also learned that this same man had changed his name to Ram Dass and was teaching ways to expand consciousness without the use of drugs. I was sold. I bought his book *Be Here Now* and devoured its contents. In no time at all, I was doing yoga, practicing meditation, eating vegetarian meals and developing a prayer discipline.

That phase of my life ended like many others. I kept some of the ideas I learned and discarded others. I still practice a few of the spiritual techniques, but others have gone by the wayside. My method of prayer has changed, but not the discipline I bring to it. Overall, that period was the beginning of my developing a spiritual philosophy of life and educating my faith. To this day, I am grateful for the experience. It changed the course of my life.

The Evolutionary Principle and Mind

Nature has done a marvelous job. It has given us the tools that we need to survive in this world. Our bodies' resilience is truly a marvel, and so is our capacity to think. Yet, there is more to us than the capacity to survive. In fact, we will survive until we die. Survival is constant. We do not have to worry about it, yet we do. Why is that? What drives us beyond our comfort levels? What makes it so difficult for us to accept life as it is? Why do we keep pushing ourselves at such a rapid rate?

I believe that we are hardwired for progress and expansion. Along with our survival skills comes the urge to improve our quality of life. For most of us, it is simply not enough to accept the status quo. We seem to have a biological imperative that pushes us beyond our personal frontiers. It is what I call the "evolutionary principle." From the earliest single-celled organisms to the more complex life forms of today, life has been driven by evolution. Life continues to evolve in an increasingly complex pattern. The evolutionary principle exists within every form of creation, and is most evident in human beings. We may not be physically evolving, but our consciousness is certainly evolving—often at an unprecedented speed.

The evolutionary principle behaves according to predictable patterns, which scientists continue to identify. These predictable patterns suggest that the evolutionary principle has "intelligence." Therefore, an intelligent vehicle is needed to drive the principle. I call that vehicle "Mind." This vehicle has a unique dual nature. It is both infinite (it has always existed and will always exist), and finite (it is measurable in living things). When referring to Mind's infinite nature, I capitalize the word because Mind is a specialized function of God.

Mind is the connecting mechanism between life's evolutionary principle and life's manifested forms. It is both infinite and finite. It is involved and invested in every manifested form, yet it is not limited by any of its manifested forms. Clearly, its substance is spirit, and many scientists are considering it as an accurate model for God.

Mind is contained in all of creation, yet it is not bound by that creation. Mind is also both responsible for *and* responsive to the evolutionary principle. This means that all forms are guided by the evolutionary principle of Mind, yet they also have a choice about how, when and where they use it. All of creation has inherited some degree of Mind's intelligence, whether it is evident at any particular moment or not. Forms have choice according to their current level of evolution. Consequently, the more evolved the form, the more expanded its choices.

For example, a plant will have fewer reproductive options than an animal, which in turn will have fewer than humans will. Since faith plays a key role in what we choose, as humans we have influence in the evolutionary process for our planet, the entire cosmos and ourselves.

Our level of faith influences Mind's effect on us. At the finite, form level Mind manifests as "our mind." It contains our intellect, i.e., our capacity to judge, rationalize, categorize, plan and project, but it also contains unconscious, mechanical functions, such as our heartbeat, our breathing, our dreaming, etc. Additionally, our minds guide our creative urge and emotions, which in its ultimate form is pure generative energy—the source of our intuition and love. In some mysterious and magical way, our minds, through the power vested in them by Mind, are responsible for all aspects of our lives. Thus, Mind is all we are. By attempting to know Mind, its spiritual essence and its evolutionary urge, we come to understand the purpose of our lives. It requires faith to pursue this venture, for Mind cannot be fully defined. Nor is it completely definable.

The evolutionary function of Mind is best accessed with a hopeful, expectant and faith-filled mind. When we come to understand the creative and loving power of Mind, we can then relax into its awesome influence and guidance. We can rest assured that it will work through our minds, in thought, emotion and body, to make us aware of its ultimate purpose for us. No aspect of our lives can escape its influence, for it is always available regardless of our venture or desire. The more we use it by exercising choice, or the more we allow it to use us by exercising intuitive guidance, the more confidence we will gain in its availability. Let me tell you a story as an illustration.

The lease on our church building was terminating. We had spoken to the landlord on several occasions about purchasing the building, but it was simply out of our financial reach. We created a committee to explore other options, but nothing better emerged. At the same time, I received a strong intuitive message that we were to remain in the building. The committee, however, was considering buying property elsewhere.

We all prayed a great deal. Finally, at one of the committee meetings, a member revealed that she knew someone who was interested in lending the church the down payment for the building—for the ridiculously low interest rate of 6 percent. There was one stipulation: The person wanted to remain anonymous. Everyone was amazed! We immediately started negotiations with the landlord. At first I thought he would not sell the building. After all, he had a terrific tenant (us!) who always accepted his rent increases. But he agreed to sell. He also agreed to a market analysis of the property in order to determine a fair price. When this was done, we made an offer slightly below what the appraisal had estimated. He accepted our offer. The entire process was a miracle from beginning to end.

This story reveals how powerful focused faith can be. We just knew that God would support our venture. That confidence came from the group's reliance on the creativity of Mind and our shared identity in it. To this day, we do not know who the individual is who lent the money, nor does it matter. Mind binds us all, and we must never be surprised by the miracles in our lives.

FAITH ENHANCER

In your journal, describe a creative venture or project you would like to complete in the future. If you have a prayer or support group, share these plans and ask them to pray with you for a successful outcome. Encourage your support team to share with you any insights they may receive during prayer.

God as a Partner

We have now seen the importance of your having a philosophy to live by. I hope that it will help you identify the cosmos and yourselves as Mind, or the expression of the evolutionary principle. It is from this basic philosophy that the categories in the matrix that correspond to an educated faith emerge. The first, and most important, is seeing God as a partner. The evolutionary principle, working as Mind, needs partners in order to further its purpose. Life has been evolving on our planet from a gaseous state to minerals, to plants and to animals. As far as we know, this has not only been an expansion of the complexity of the cellular structure, but also of the consciousness of each stage. In other words, each stage is more conscious, more aware of its choices. We are now at the stage of evolution where we can consciously participate in it. Through our choices, we can expedite or delay the evolutionary process. We have become co-creative partners with God.

With an educated faith, we learn to minimize our perceptions of an authoritative God and embrace the challenges and responsibilities that come from co-creation. Recognizing that we are full participants in the creation of our lives can be both exciting and frightening. It is exciting to invest ourselves in the outcomes of our visions and intentions—for in so doing, we come to know God and ourselves more intimately. The fear is about our accepting responsibility for *all* the circumstances in our lives—not just the ones that please us. When God is accepted as a partner, the relationship demands trust. Having left behind a God of whims and moods, our copartnership is consistent. We accept that God works in definite ways. We come to know, without a doubt, that we hold in our conscious mind the power of the evolutionary principle. We must come to know that what we envision for ourselves is not only good for us, but for the entire cosmos.

In my young adulthood, during a particularly painful and depressed time in my life, I became suicidal and self-destructive. I lived in constant fear that my behavior would result in death, even though my feelings of despair wished it at some level. I was drinking and drugging heavily, driving fast cars and engaging in reckless behavior. It culminated in a car accident where one of the individuals involved died. I was badly hurt, as my face smashed into the dashboard and required surgery. It was at this desperate juncture (it often requires such extreme conditions) that I decided to make a partnership with God. I agreed to dedicate my entire life to the pursuit of God, in exchange for having God tell me when my moment for death would be. That agreement, to this day, brings me great peace and relief. God and I are in a co-creative partnership about my life and death.

There are infinite amounts of partnership that can, and ought, to be created with God through Mind. Another vital one for me is my marriage. My marriage is based on the principle that God, as Mind, binds my wife and I. This means that whenever our human resources fail to resolve a particular disagreement, we turn to our larger Mind for assistance and guidance. For almost thirty years, it has worked. We have a vibrant, refreshing and grounded relationship that continues to feed us individually and collectively.

FAITH ENHANCER

In your journal, compose a partnership agreement with your God. Be concise, but be daring. Although this process may feel uncomfortable and scary, remember it is your right to claim your divine inheritance.

Trusting the Law of Cause and Effect

One of the main sources of help for educating our faith is understanding the "law of cause and effect"—or simply, the Law. (The word is capitalized to indicate the infinite or absolute component of this function of Mind.) While this Law has many applications in Newtonian physics, psychology, religion and sociology, I learned about the Law in the playgrounds where I grew up. Simply stated, the Law goes something like this: *What goes around, comes around.* In my childhood playgrounds, I learned about social justice, psychological deviancy and the laws of physics in one swift lesson: *You will be treated in the same manner as you treat others.* As I grew older, it was a short mental hop to understanding how the Law deals with all of creation. Maturity has demonstrated that I am responsible for my life. Whether I like it or not, my life unfolds according to the choices that I make. Although the choices I have to make are not always easy or clear, with courage and hindsight, I see how my choices shape my life.

Where do my choices come from? Some say that choices are the selections we make from what the environment offers. Upon initial investigation, it may seem so. However, if we are willing to look beneath the surface, we find an entire spectrum of creation that goes deeper. From observing my own life, I propose that we choose from options that are of our own selection. In other words, all our choices are in some way the creation of our intention. What I mean is that what I call my life is the summation of all of my previous choices. A previous "choice" provides the "effect" for the next "cause," and so on. Yet where does the initial "cause" come from? This question has some metaphysical implications that are beyond the scope of this text. But a practical place to start is by looking at the choices that we made in adolescence—or that were made for us in childhood. Our childhood history, and the primal philosophy that we formulated then, continue to play out in our choices today. The "causes" of our childhood continue to have power in our lives, that are often used unconsciously.

A personal story may help to illustrate this process. One of the "themes" (as I call them) of my childhood was to gain control of those around me. As the youngest of four siblings who were close in age, I constantly felt at a disadvantage. All my siblings had an advantage over me in terms of stature, knowledge, experience and parental access. I desperately wanted to control them, and this created a primal philosophy for the rest of my life. This passion for control of others displayed itself early on. My mother reports that she received complaints from the kindergarten teacher, a most loving nun, about my escapades. It seemed that I had a natural gift for attracting peers and forming them into "gangs." The gang would do as I instructed it. Often, they would terrorize others in the playground. Thus began one of my original "causes." With maturity, it would become my gift for leadership but also my tendency to be authoritarian.

Over time, I have come to recognize this tendency as the result of the law of cause and effect. I have also gained insight into its original "cause." In a raw, unconscious and uneducated way, the gift of leadership is the result of my intentions to gain control over my environment. If left unconscious and uneducated, it has the potential to influence all of the choices that I make today in a negative way. For instance, all my jobs as an adult—including my current one—have carried the potential for leadership. This has placed me in a position of controlling others. By educating my faith, however, I am learning to let go of my instinctual need to control others. It is a challenging process, and the possibility of success increases—as I become a copartner with God.

There are deeper ramifications to this Law. For ages, the wisdom teachers have made us aware of an infinite creative process that is happening through each and every one of us. These teachers traditionally have been philosophers, mystics, prophets and seers. However, most recently, this group has included motivational teachers and business consultants. Whatever their title, these wisdom teachers are all saying the same thing: *There is a creative law that responds to each thought. This creative law enacts our thoughts and intentions. It puts into play what "goes around" and then it also "brings it around."*

As we learn more about our faith and become more aware of ourselves, we can experience the evolutionary principle in a more conscious fashion. In doing so, we can instigate the law of cause and effect more intentionally. There is something very exciting about recognizing the creative power that is our divine inheritance. Simultaneously, this awareness demands that we take responsibility for our lives.

FAITH ENHANCER

In your journal, identify some of your childhood patterns that instigate the law of cause and effect in your life today. Give solid examples.

Affirming Our Personal Good

Along with the gift of faith, we are each born with the gift of awareness. Awareness is not intelligence per se. It is not about how smart we are. Awareness is our capacity to pay attention and learn about the messages we receive from our environment and ourselves. It makes it possible to live a life of self-reflection. Often, just the mere activity of looking at our thoughts, our feelings, our behaviors, our visions and ourselves sets us on the journey of faith restoration. I am not sure why this is. It may have to do with our natural capacity for love and creativity. Once we see rightly, healing begins. This awareness can emerge as knowledge of our history, family themes and personality patterns. Although this psychological knowledge may restore our natural faith, it will not enhance it. Eventually, we must affirm our good.

The historical experiences that rob us of our natural faith are stored as beliefs. They have become the credo through which we perceive, choose and create our lives. They work as a personal law, producing the same results repeatedly. However, we can restructure those beliefs by "planting" new beliefs in their place. The Law, which is the medium of the evolutionary principle, is not bound by history. It is infinite, but also works through our personal law. Therefore, it will respond to our intentions. Consequently, once we are aware of a particular belief that is sabotaging our good, we can immediately affirm a higher good instead, and the Law will respond automatically. This will institute a renewed personal law.

When affirming our good, it is important that the statements we make or intentions we set are genuine and make sense to us. In other words, if we have to "brainwash" ourselves into embracing our innate goodness, it is entirely possible that we are embracing someone else's concept of what is good. We cannot rush the re-creation of our belief systems and start implanting what simply *looks* good. As we become aware of our history, emotions and thoughts, our faith will mature, and we will gain confidence in our creative skills. Thus when it comes time to affirm our good, we will wait to be gently guided from within. The first step is to become aware of the old beliefs that no longer serve us. The second step is to implant a set of new beliefs that affirm a higher good. The third step is to verbalize these new beliefs. Either through prayer or intentional conversation, our spoken word has tremendous power to restore our faith. Our verbal affirmations of "good" will either neutralize the old, fearful beliefs, or replace them with better ones.

The Law works automatically in our lives. If we are intent on change, the natural gifts of awareness and faith will be abundant—and more than sufficient to help us change. Our part is to continue declaring our willingness to change, and remaining vigilant about watching out for old beliefs that may sabotage our good. In some ways, it is nothing more than a game we play. If we do not take ourselves too seriously, change can be easy and fun. Of course, some beliefs are based on serious trauma, and we may require professional help. Regardless of what those beliefs are, however, the Law will apply to them in the same manner. Affirm your good, and the Law will find you.

FAITH ENHANCER

What longstanding belief would you like to change? In your journal, write down an affirmation that will neutralize that belief. Pray your affirmation daily. Be bold. Trust the Law to do the work.

A Life of Expectancy

We have seen how an educated faith requires an all-encompassing philosophy of life. This philosophy includes acknowledging the evolution of the cosmos and of the individual, and understanding that the current evolution is one of consciousness. It demands that we bring into the light those personal, racial and cultural themes that lie in our dark unconscious.

At this level of faith, God is seen as a partner who co-creates with us in the evolution of the cosmos. Learning to trust God and Mind comes with understanding the Law—a gift from God that encourages us to be conscious beings. The more conscious we are, the more in tune we will be with our purpose here on Earth. We begin to see that the patterns in our lives are a series of cause-and-effect events grounded in our thinking patterns.

At this stage of faith, awareness alone—simply paying attention to what happens around us—can restore our optimism and hope. Our losses of faith no longer paralyze us. We never have to operate in the dark. We enjoy a life of *expectancy*. Note that the concept of "expectancy" is quite different from that of "expectation." Expectation involves looking for specific results in which we are emotionally invested. Expectancy is a beneficial state of mind that encourages optimism and joy as we think to ourselves, *I wonder what delightful ending this event will have?* This attitude of joyful expectancy is also called "nonattachment," and is a wonderfully congenial way to move through life.

FAITH ENHANCER

Start a meditation practice if you have not done so already. Begin meditating for five minutes a day, and gradually increase your time as you become comfortable with the process. Paying attention to your breath—as you slowly breathe in and out—will relax your body and mind. Of course you will be distracted by a variety of thoughts. In fact, meditation is an excellent way to discover what your mind is "up to." Old belief patterns may be revealed, and gentle guidance will be offered. You can also use affirmative prayers together with meditation. When a frightening thought or image arises in your consciousness, immediately move into affirmative prayer. You will make terrific gains in neutralizing old belief patterns and creating new ones.

CHAPTER SIX

Enlightened Faith

> There is a Principle which is the basis of things, which all speech aims to say, and all action to evolve, a simple, quiet, undescribed, and undescribable Presence, dwelling very peacefully in us, our rightful Lord: we are not to do, but to let do; not to work, but to be worked upon; and to this homage there is a consent of all thoughtful and just men in all ages and conditions.
>
> —*Ralph Waldo Emerson*

An educated faith teaches us to see God as a partner and to use our mind as the creative vehicle for the evolutionary principle. Both of these concepts are most useful in developing an effective, faith-filled life. Through this empowerment, we come to know ourselves as divine beings, having a specific purpose. Our faith grows as our trust in God deepens. We come to trust the Law and the power of our affirmative words. We recognize that a life of conscious intention surpasses one of unconscious negligence.

The growth of our faith does not stop here. Though this is a comfortable place to live, it is not the end of our spiritual journey. Our faith can take another leap to the level of enlightenment, where few individuals dwell. All of us, however, have spent brief moments there. During enlightened faith, we are able to see the total perfection of all things. This is the faith that allows us to *be* rather than just *do*.

Enlightened faith deals with an aspect of God that lies beyond reason and analysis. This faith is based on our willingness to accept the paradox that life engenders. This stage of faith does not focus on right or wrong, good or bad, more or less. We are now talking about simply *being* with what is and learning to see its perfection. This is an accurate definition of love, or the love of God. This level of faith moves us to suspend judgment. Over time, we notice that our judgments have lessened; behaviors and people that plagued us in the past no longer bother us. At the enlightened stage, God begins to work magic on *you*.

The Trained Mind Surrenders

The evolution of our faith has trained our minds to acknowledge the natural faith with which we were born. We have set and accomplished goals and objectives. We have reconstructed our belief system and perhaps neutralized our traumatic history. We have also developed a new relationship with God. Our minds have been empowered to learn and be effective in using conscious thought as a creative vehicle. We have elevated our faith through our education and have discovered God as a copartner in life. Through this understanding, we find God willingly at our service. But hold on: enlightened faith now asks that we surrender all this!

Contradictory as it may sound, our faith can grow beyond the educated level. That growth, however, will demand that we stop trying to change the circumstances in our lives—enlightened faith sees all circumstances as "perfect." Everything is strategically designed to bring a new level of consciousness to our minds. Our minds suddenly become conduits through which the evolutionary principle communicates with us and the world. Therefore, as paradoxical as it may seem, the empowered mind begins to release its grip on its desires and starts to accept all of its perceptions as "good."

There is a deep sense of humility that comes with this transformation. Surrendering is not easy for our mind since it likes to be in charge. The entire function of our personal law is to help us survive and thrive. It does this best by establishing a strong identity that is accompanied by an equally strong sense of self-esteem. A trained faith greatly assists this development, and it is not easy for the mind to relinquish its role. In fact, it won't. Surrendering doesn't happen through will power, but through the power of enlightened faith. Enlightened faith can only be accomplished by deepening our relationship with God. That happens when we naturally surrender our conscious goals and objectives to the highest will—God. The mystics have always known this. "Not my will, but Thy will be done" is an ancient refrain that hints at this surrender. Enlightened faith operates in the realm of the soul, not the intellect.

Living the Goodness of Life

An enlightened faith starts with the premise that all of life is whole and complete. This faith assures us that God is ever present, and that God's presence makes good all that is. Even when we cannot see it, we come to trust in the goodness of our reality and that of others. This can be most challenging. For example, my students often ask, "Where was God during the Holocaust?" I do not know the answer to that question—or many others like it. I do not even claim to acknowledge the presence of God in my life at all times, let alone in the lives of others.

The challenge for those who want to train their faith is to express a *willingness* to see life's goodness, even when it seems hidden. The concept of being *willing* carries the connotation that although one may not feel ready, one will still embrace shifts of perception. Enlightened faith requires surrender, both for a specific result and a specific time. A great deal of discipline is required of us, and it will not happen simply because we wish it or will it. The perception of wholeness evolves in its own time, and only as our faith expands into higher levels. Remember that this level of faith is not one that we choose. On the contrary, it chooses us. If you *think* you are in an enlightened level of faith, that's a sure sign that you are not!

An enlightened faith poses some unique dilemmas. If one perceives all of life as good, why act when action seems needed? Indeed, there is a very real danger for "pseudo-mystics" *not* to act when they should, because they believe "everything is perfect." Beware of such an attitude. When we study the lives of mystics and saints, we learn that they were deeply involved in compassionate works of charity. In seeing the wholeness and goodness of life, they also saw that all of life was interdependent. This interdependence demanded that they be responsible world citizens.

I remember such a moment when applying for ministerial school. I sat in front of the admissions panel that was in charge of evaluating my intention. They asked the obvious question: "Why are you here?" I gave the answer no thought; it just shot out from my soul. "I have no choice," I said. They looked puzzled and responded, "But we all have choices." I said, "No, you do not understand. When it comes to my ministry, I don't have a choice. This is something that is happening to me. I am simply along for the ride." So it has been for the past eleven years. Just when I find myself overwhelmed by the circumstances of my ministry, and I want to take control, I find that the only solution is to surrender. It is not always easy, but it is very simple.

FAITH ENHANCER

What is the purpose of your life? Is there an ideal, belief, circumstance or event for which you would surrender everything? If not, it may be time for you to set an intention to discover that one thing which requires your total surrender. Write down your thoughts in your journal.

Wisdom Through Intuition and Revelation

I have a friend who has surrendered his life to God. He is as close to being a mystic as any person that I know. Of course, he would be the last to accept that title, so I won't mention his name. He is also one of the most creative individuals I know. He takes tremendous risks in his career, and he once resigned from a high-paying job to live in isolation with a teacher in order to study a mystical path. His spiritual practices are solitude and silence. His quest is to make all of his life a spiritual practice. He recently told me that he no longer tries to make rational decisions. He will only do what his intuitive inner guidance tells him. He has come to trust in his intuition to the degree that he has little use for his rational mind. When these intuitive messages come, regardless of how far out they may be, he follows them. They often take him to many parts of the world, and they place a great strain on his life. Yet, his life is full and fulfilled.

Enlightened faith demands total trust in one's relationship with God. This faith knows that Mind will guide us in every situation, regardless of how complex or simple. To know that we are in constant relationship with God is to know that God will not fail us. Mind will always provide the direction we need to take. Our job is to remain patient, pray and keep our mind open to receive. What gets in the way of our intuition is the constant rattle that we entertain in our minds. Once that is silenced, the rest is up to God.

FAITH ENHANCER

During one of your meditation periods, sit with pen and paper on your lap. Jot down as many of your thoughts as you can. Do not be judgmental and let them flow. Don't attempt to solve any problems that present themselves. Simply jot them down. You will discover the barriers that keep your intuition from emerging.

Divine Right Action

A delightful woman worked for me for a few years. Her natural faith was admirable. When someone would inquire as to her state of health, she would respond, "I am divine!" When things would get fouled up and she would feel befuddled, her immediate reaction was, "All is in divine right action." Her faith supported her lifestyle. She did house-sitting at a million-dollar home, thus allowing her to work part time and devote the rest of her time to writing. I mention this story, not because this person has an enlightened faith (though she may well have), but because the mystic comes to accept the synchronicity of life. Knowing and trusting in the wholeness of life, the person with an enlightened faith knows that there is nothing out of order. There are neither accidents nor coincidences. Life is lived in a constant state of knowing and accepting. All is in divine right action.

We are all capable of being mystics. Our minds have been "hardwired" for that likelihood. I call it the mystical aspect of mind. Simply put, it is the mind's ability to be in the moment. Being aware of the moment is the experience that Eastern religions call "witnessing." The mystical aspect of the mind easily moves into a place of detachment, and detachment allows perception without judgment. It can only be mastered when one is grounded in the wholeness and perfection of life. To be deeply rooted in divine right action is to acknowledge that all of the events that surround us, even the ones that do not seem to fit, have their place in the evolution of our life. The mystical mind witnesses all that is happening, but remains focused on the good.

My students often ask me whether they should watch the news or read a newspaper. They fear that such worldly material will contaminate their thinking and threaten their faith. Though this may indeed be true, the goal of the mystic is to be able to observe the world and hold on to what is true—that is, "To be in the world, but not of it." One of my favorite teachers in ministerial school would say, "If you don't watch the news, how do you know what to pray for?" Enlightened faith connects us to a universal wisdom that allows us to know divine right action in all existence. This "knowing" is more than an intellectual knowing, but a heartfelt connection with all that is. It is recognition of the interdependence among all individuals and their circumstances.

FAITH ENHANCER

Go to a spot where there is lots of activity. Perhaps it is your favorite park, a playground or a sidewalk where people stroll. Sit on one of the benches and simply witness what is happening. Make no judgments. If you find yourself in judgment, take a few deep breaths and return to your witnessing.

Contemplation, Grace and Bliss

For the mystic, life happens through grace. Grace is a gift from God that has a most beneficial effect on our lives. The mystic does not take credit for any results in life. It is all God's doing. It is all God's grace. It unfolds for the benefit of the highest good of everyone involved. No one individual gets credit. Life is simply the heavenly evolution of God. The religious tool of the mystic is contemplation. Contemplation is to observe without judgment. It is to deliberately suspend opinions and simply be present for the beauty and the power of *what is*. This is not an easy concept for the normal mind. We always want to analyze, categorize and rearrange.

I make a habit of spending a couple of weeks each year in our summer home. It is located on top of a mountain and can only be reached through a treacherous, four-wheel-drive road. It fronts some of the most isolated wilderness in New Mexico. Only an occasional plane and the buzzing of the hummingbirds disturb the absolute stillness. I go alone, with the commitment to not listen to the radio, talk on the telephone or connect myself with the world in any superfluous way.

On one particular trip, I spent a great deal of time hiking in the wilderness. By tiring my body, my mind entered a quiet state that invited "witnessing." Suddenly I noticed that my "normal" way of perceiving had shifted. I felt completely connected to my surroundings. There was no separation between the environment and me. As I continued on the trail, I came across a mother bear with two cubs. Wildlife lore teaches that bears will usually scamper when meeting humans—except when they feel their young are threatened. Though this thought briefly crossed my mind, my current state of faith would not allow me to dwell on it. What I did was to simply watch her and marvel at her beauty. I became enthralled by her motherly ways, and instead of perceiving her as foe, she and her family became a part of me.

We passed each other without incident, and to this day I do not know whether she noticed me at all.

That was a moment of bliss for me. It stayed with me for a long time. It eventually came to reside as a memory that now fuels my hunger for enlightened faith. I have come to accept that we all have a mystical aspect. We all have the capacity to experience bliss and the possibility of enlightened faith. These moments of bliss, whether reached in sexual orgasm, strenuous activity, the accomplishment of a goal or being present to the moment, stimulate our desire for an enlightened faith.

I have found it difficult, or nearly impossible, to remain in this mystical state of "witnessing." My daily perceptions are usually reactive and they place me in a position of separation and judgment. I tend to judge the events and people around me. I create concepts that my mind is able to understand and eventually categorize. This is the mind's tendency to seek survival and create pseudo-safety. I say "pseudo" because eventually some other circumstance will arrive to dislodge our previous concepts, and the mind's reorganization will begin all over again. We must come to understand that the reorganization of all concepts in the mind will always fall short of the mystical process. We cannot use logic or rationalization to reach the mystical mind. Only when we surrender to God, or higher Mind, will we taste the nectar of intuition and grace.

It helps me to immerse myself in my spiritual practices. They remind me not to get entrenched in judgmental thinking. I also surround myself with friends and professionals who know the higher truth of who and what we are. I hold dear many friends who encourage me to withstand the distractions of judgment and separation. The intellectual mind stubbornly resists the mystical mind. Still, we all have the capacity to bypass the intellect's stubbornness. In fact, that capacity is a gift from the divine. Some call it "grace." I have always assumed that grace is the result of the spiritual saturation that accumulates over years of spiritual practice. Other individuals, however, swear that their "salvation" was an intervention of grace. Such was the case for John Newton, the sea captain who for years had been running slaves from Africa to the New World. During a particular stormy trip, he saw the error of his enterprise. He abandoned the lucrative business and dedicated his life to serving God. One of his first endeavors was to write the lyrics of the well-known hymn, "Amazing Grace."

We do not have to wait for a "stormy trip" to have grace in our lives. Nor do we have to be fully saturated in spiritual practices in order to experience grace. Grace can visit us at any time, whether to change the course of our lives or to simply inspire us with a new idea or a heightened sense of love. All that is required is that we "lean" toward God whenever our lives are challenged. Our daily discipline of spiritual practices will open the doors to grace. Once grace is in place in our lives, we can fall into blissful repose.

FAITH ENHANCER

Schedule a spiritual retreat for yourself—an overnight trip, if possible, where there are few distractions. Go alone, remain in solitude and take a vow of silence. Bring with you only a book of inspiration and your journal. Spend your time listening to God.

CONCLUSION

The whole object of the universe to us
is the formation of character. If you think you came
into being for the purpose of taking an important part
in the administration of events, to guard a province
of moral creation from ruin, and that its salvation
hangs on the success of your single arm, you
have wholly mistaken your business.

—Ralph Waldo Emerson

Faith is a dynamic phenomenon. It can be lost and regained. It shrinks and expands. Sometimes it seems to elude us; other times it is unshakable. We seem to have faith in certain areas of our lives, while we lack it in others. Our faith, more than anything else, affects our confidence, optimism and hope. It is in our best interest to learn about it and apply the results of our investigation to our lives.

We have learned that we all come into the world with a natural faith. This immature faith is sufficient to move us through the most difficult circumstances. It is immature in that it relies on outer forces to influence the course of our lives. Nevertheless, it is a faith of sorts and brings us some relief and sustenance during the difficult periods of our lives.

This natural faith can be lost, however. Hardship, trauma, reversals and betrayals influence the quantity and quality of the faith that we place on the outer world and in a God that exists outside of ourselves. Certainly, faith in other human beings can be swayed by their behavior. When we are disappointed by an unmet expectation, a certain amount of faith is lost. When an atrocity in the world occurs, our faith in the benevolence of God may erode. These challenges are inevitable. Yet our faith can be regained, perhaps not to be the same naive faith dependent on an outside reality, but a stronger, inner faith in our human and spiritual qualities and capabilities. This is a maturational process that can be instigated on our part. We can build the "spiritual muscles" necessary to confront the disappointing events that befall us. These muscles will eventually form our character and our ways of perceiving and surviving life's catastrophes.

There is an educated faith that emerges as we learn

about our human and spiritual makeup. Through analyzing our beliefs, our identities and our experiences, we come to know more about ourselves. Since much of this material is unconscious, it is the primary factor that affects the response to our circumstances. In other words, it influences the amount of faith we may have at any particular time. By learning about ourselves, we can develop a mature and sustainable faith. We must not only learn about our human makeup, but about our spiritual nature as well. An educated faith has us learn about our ultimate connection with Mind or God. In doing so, our faith stands on a secure relationship with Spirit rather than on mere wishes and hopes.

The education of our faith includes scripture study; inspirational readings; investigating scientific research; prayer; meditation; and any other spiritual practices that assist us in learning about our human and divine natures. We can be inspired by the example of others or motivated by journeys others have dared. At times, we may even be overwhelmed by the sheer excitement of the moment. Nevertheless, we stay true to our own journey. The result of such a discipline is an enlightened faith. This level of faith allows us to accept any particular circumstance with a sense of peace and joy. We participate in the moment and suspend our judgments. We see beauty in everything and accept our fellow human beings for their true worth. We embrace all seeming opposites, the "good" and "bad," as the necessary make-up of our spiritual journey.

Enlightened faith is rare. When we experience it, it takes our breath away. It places us in a space of wholeness and oneness with our surroundings. It makes everything fall into place. Rare as these moments may be, however, we must pursue them as if our lives depended on them. This is because they do! One of the reasons enlightened faith is rare is because we must travel that faith journey alone. No particular dogma or system of worship will automatically produce an enlightened result. They will definitely help, but it is not until we totally embrace our divinity that enlightenment becomes the norm.

I will finish with a sequel to my sister's story (see page 15). Although she had to accept that her body would not bear a pregnancy and childbirth, she refused to relinquish the idea of being a mother. She went to work on this idea with the same spiritual diligence she applied to her healing. She pursued adoption, and she learned about the many obstacles that older adoptive parents face. She was telling her story to someone on a plane, and this person expressed a desire to help her. Through a series of miraculous events, she heard of a young, pregnant mother in a foreign country who was unable to parent her baby. My sister flew in for the birth. She was present at the very moment that her baby girl arrived in this world. Despite horrendous bureaucratic mix-ups in this foreign country—including threats to send the newborn to an orphanage and demands that she adopt an older child instead—my sister persisted in her faith. She eventually brought her adopted daughter to this country where she raises her in full health. My sister's faith prevailed again.

Testing Your Faith

Our faith is not the same at all times. We will have times when our optimism and hope are high, and we feel like we can conquer the world. There will be other times when we are pessimistic. It helps to take a spiritual inventory and learn more about our levels of faith.

In a similar manner, our faith may be high regarding some issues, but low for others. For instance, our relationships may be in order, and we may be optimistic that they will always work out. In the financial arena, however, we may be unsure about our future and our connection to our spiritual source may be shaky. Other areas, such as health or creativity, are also worth evaluating.

On the following page, you will find a blank Evolution of Faith matrix. Select a particular topic or issue, such as health, finances or relationships. Then place check marks in the boxes that best describe your state of faith around that topic. Use the filled-in table on page 4 as a guide. The more honest you are with yourself, the more accurate your faith inventory will be.

May You Grow in Faith

Thank you for completing this book. I trust that, in some mystical and magical ways, it has helped (and will continue to help) your faith to grow. The more faith-filled you are, the happier you will be. The happier you are, the more joy everyone around you will feel. It will ultimately be a better world for us all. Thank you for making it so.

EVOLUTION OF FAITH MATRIX

Categories	Natural	Lost	Educated	Enlightened
Deity Identity				
Emotional Response				
Intellectual Activity				
Mental Participation				
Innate Reaction				
Probability Factor				
Religious Tools				
Causality				
Divine Involvement				
Reactive Pattern				

RECOMMENDED READINGS TO BUILD YOUR FAITH

You'll See It When You Believe It. Wayne W. Dyer. Quill, 2001.

Conversations with God. Neale Donald Walsh. Putnam Publishing, 1996.

The Seven Spiritual Laws of Success. Deepak Chopra. Amber-Allen Pub., 1995.

The Science of Mind. Ernest Holmes. J. P. Tarcher, 1998.

Selected Writings of Ralph Waldo Emerson. Modern Library, 1992.

Original Blessing. Matthew Fox. Putnam Publishing, 2000.

Callings: Finding and Following an Authentic Life. Gregg Lavoy. Three Rivers Press, 1998.

Happiness Is a Serious Problem. Dennis Prager. Regan Books, 1999.

Becoming a Practical Mystic. Jacquelyn Small. Quest Books, 1998.

Care of the Soul. Thomas Moore. Harper Perennial, 1994.

Mysticism. Evelyn Underhill. Oneworld Publications, 1999.

Chicken Soup for the Soul. Jack Canfield and Mark Victor Hansen. Deerfield Beach, FL. Health Communications, Inc., 1995.

Spiritual Economics. Eric Butterworth. Unity, 2001.

The 7 Habits of Highly Effective People. Stephen R. Covey. Simon & Schuster, 1990.

Journey of Awakening. Ram Dass: Bantam Books, 1990.

The Practice of the Presence of God. Brother Lawrence: Fleming H. Revell Co., 1999.

ABOUT THE AUTHOR

Reverend Bernardo Monserrat was born in Havana, Cuba. He emigrated to the United States and lived with foster parents until his parents reclaimed him one year later. He has university degrees in mathematics, counseling and philosophy. Prior to doing his graduate work, he completed a tour in the Peace Corps. He has been married to Dr. Catherine for twenty-eight years, and together, they have raised two children, written a workbook to assist couples enhance their intimacy, and conduct workshops on creating spiritual relationships. They now live in Santa Fe, New Mexico, where he is the senior minister at the Church of Religious Science. He is a spiritual coach and serves clients from all over the world.

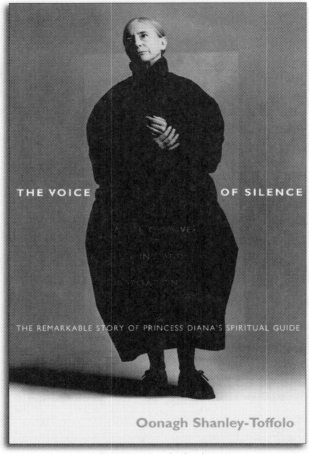

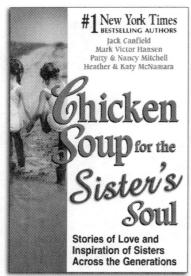

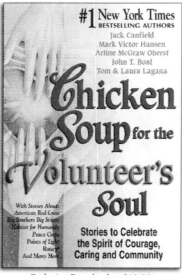